WORLD BOOK
looks at
INVENTIONS AND DISCOVERIES

World Book, Inc.
a Scott Fetzer Company
Chicago London Sydney Toronto

WORLD BOOK
looks at
INVENTIONS AND DISCOVERIES

World Book looks at
Books in this series are based on information and illustrations contained in The World Book Encyclopedia.

Created and edited by Brian Williams and Brenda Williams.
Designed by Tim Mayer.

World Book, Inc.
525 W. Monroe
Chicago, Illinois 60661

For information on other World Book products, call 1-800-255-1750 x3771.

ISBN 0-7166-1802-8 (hard cover)
ISBN 0-7166-1808-7 (soft cover)
Library of Congress Catalog Card Number 96-62477

Printed in Mexico

1 2 3 4 5 6 7 8 9 10 99 98 97 96

CONTENTS

Inventions and Discoveries   4

Why People Invent   6

How People Invent   12

Early Inventions   20

The Spread of Knowledge   22

The Age of Ideas   24

Newton and a New World   28

The Industrial Revolution   30

Factories   32

Machines on the Farm   34

Steam on Rails,
Steam at Sea   36

Steam on the Road   38

People on Wheels   40

Dots, Dashes,
and Snapshots   42

Electricity Switches On   44

The Great Inventor   46

Waves Through Space   48

Medical Progress   50

The Electronic Revolution   52

Flying High   54

The History of Invention   56

Glossary   62

Index   63

Inventions and Discoveries

Inventors and discoverers have changed people's lives throughout history. Many of the things we use every day – this book included – are the result of thousands of years of invention and discovery.

Invention or discovery?

When something that already exists in nature is noticed or recognized for the first time, we call it a discovery. Many such discoveries are made by scientists. An invention is the creation of something that never existed before. For example, when ancient people saw natural forest fires burning, they discovered fire. They learned how to make their own fires by using a burning branch to light a pile of dry sticks. Later, people invented matches and other ways of making fire. Look around, and you will see inventions everywhere.

Changing our lives

Thousands of years ago, people lived by hunting animals and gathering wild plants.

From stone arrowheads to space rockets. Stone Age people chipped arrowheads into leaf shapes and triangle shapes. It took many thousands of years for people to improve on this simple technology. Until the 1940's, space rockets like the Atlas-Centaur satellite launcher were known only in science fiction stories.

Some inventions develop quickly. The first practical single-rotor helicopter (left) was built and flown by Igor Sikorsky in 1939. Within 10 years, the helicopter was a familiar sight in the skies. It is now being developed in new ways. A tilt-rotor helicopter (right) can fly like a conventional helicopter or a propeller aircraft.

The wheel was one of the most important inventions in history. The wheels on this wagon from the A.D. 1000's (left) are not very different from those on the delivery wagon of the early 1900's (right). But the air-filled rubber tires on the later vehicle undoubtedly made for a smoother ride.

To find food, they had to move from place to place. About 9000 B.C., people began to grow their own crops and raise animals such as sheep, goats, and cattle. They had invented farming, and no longer had to wander in search of food. Now people could settle in villages.

Much later came the Industrial Revolution of the 1700's, with such inventions as the steam engine and new machines in factories. The Industrial Revolution brought another great change in the way people lived, as they moved from farms to the cities to work in factories. Change still affects our lives today, as we move through the electronic and communication revolutions.

In this book

In this book you will learn how some of the world's great inventions and discoveries were made, and how they affected people's lives. We need to go on inventing and discovering, to solve the many problems that the world faces today. So this is a story that has no end!

Puzzled by a new word?

To learn the meaning of a difficult or new word, turn to the glossary on page 62.

Good or bad?

Many inventions have made life better for people, but some, such as weapons of war, have been harmful. Other inventions have had both good and bad effects. The automobile, for example, has:

- given people a fast, convenient means of travel,

- created jobs for many workers,

- hurt and killed people in traffic accidents,

- jammed city streets,

- contributed to air pollution.

Why People Invent

John Kay, inventor of the flying shuttle.

People invent things for several reasons. Some inventors are driven by curiosity, some have an urge to create, and some hope to make money. Most inventions are created to satisfy the needs of people.

Three basic needs lead to inventions and discoveries. They are economic needs, military needs, and social needs. Let's look first at how economic needs can inspire inventions.

Demand speeds supply

Before the 1700's, most manufactured goods – such as cloth – were made by people such as weavers and spinners in their own homes. They worked by hand and at their own pace. Merchants bought cloth from these home workers.

By the early 1700's, however, merchants wanted more cloth to meet a growing demand. In 1733, John Kay, an English clockmaker, invented a weaving machine called the flying shuttle. With this machine, weavers could make cloth faster than the spinners could provide them with thread. Cloth merchants then had to hire more spinners, or find a new, speedier way to spin. During the 1760's and 1770's, three English inventors – James Hargreaves, Richard Arkwright, and Samuel Crompton – invented machines to help spinners work much faster.

Now there was more thread available than weavers and weaving machines to make cloth. In the mid-1780's, Edmund Cartwright, another English inventor, invented a steam-powered weaving machine, or loom. At last the weavers could keep up with the spinners.

Before the age of factory machines, a family worked at home to make cloth, as shown in this engraving from the 1700's.

A flying shuttle loom of the 1700's. On machines like this, weavers could weave cloth much faster than before.

Mr. Whitney's cotton gin

The new machines provided great quantities of cloth at lower cost. Merchants could sell cloth at lower prices, so people bought more. The demand for raw (natural) cotton increased accordingly, and a new problem arose.

Raw cotton contains seeds that must be removed before the cotton can be used on spinning machines. Picking out the seeds was done by hand, and too slowly to keep pace with the new demand for cotton. Then, in 1793, the American inventor Eli Whitney built a machine called a cotton gin. One cotton gin could remove cotton seeds as fast as 50 people working by hand. So now the cotton growers could keep up with the spinning and weaving machines.

One invention had spurred another, and then another. And people's lives had been greatly changed.

The toothed cotton gin saved workers the task of removing cotton seeds by hand.

The cotton gin shown here is a model of the machine made by Eli Whitney in 1793.

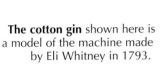

About Eli Whitney

As a teenager, Eli Whitney (1765-1825) set up a nail-making business. While studying to be a lawyer and doing odd jobs to earn his keep, he heard cotton growers complain they could not make money because of the time it took to clean the raw cotton. So Whitney invented his famous machine – the cotton gin. He could not make his machines fast enough to meet the demand. Other people copied the idea, and he took them to court to try to protect his invention. He later made muskets and other weapons for the United States government.

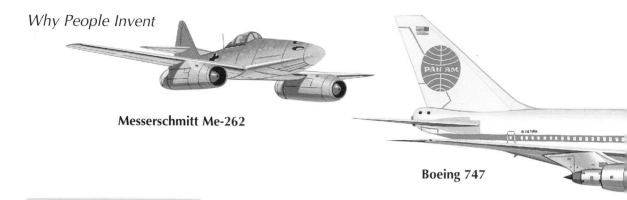

Messerschmitt Me-262

Boeing 747

What were the first guns like?

No one knows who invented the gun. Most historians believe the first guns were cannonlike weapons used by Arabs in North Africa during the 1300's. The first guns were brass or iron tubes with a small hole at the closed end for setting fire to the gunpowder.

Over the centuries, war and the threat of war have driven people to create new and ever more destructive weapons. Military needs have led to many inventions and discoveries.

Gunpowder and shot

Soldiers in ancient times fought with swords, spears, and bows and arrows – weapons that had changed little over hundreds of years. A great change came in the 1200's, with the use of gunpowder in war. People in Asia were probably the first to discover that a mixture of saltpeter, sulfur, and charcoal produced a black powder that would explode. This knowledge moved westward, and eventually changed the face of war in Europe. The stone walls of castles were no defense against rockets and cannon balls fired by gunpowder, the first practical explosive.

Chinese warriors fired gunpowder rockets in battle during the A.D. 1200's. By 1940, rocket missiles were being built. In the photograph (right), American rocket pioneer Robert H. Goddard inspects a rocket built under his supervision.

What was Greek fire?

Greek fire was a chemical mixture first used in warfare in the A.D. 600's. It burned furiously, even in water. Warriors in the Middle Ages shot Greek fire with arrows and through tubes. No one knows for sure how it was made, but it probably contained liquid petroleum thickened with resin and sulfur.

Jet planes were first used during World War II. The German Messerschmitt Me-262 – the first jet combat plane – flew missions over Europe in 1944 and 1945. After the war, jet engine technology produced passenger planes like the Boeing 747, which began service in 1970.

Two world wars

New weapons to appear during World War I (1914-1918) included the airplane, the submarine, and the tank. World War II (1939-1945) led to more research and invention than any other war, including the most destructive single weapon ever invented – the atomic bomb. Yet wartime inventions have also brought benefits. The jet engine that was first used in warplanes powered new and faster passenger planes in peacetime. And radar, an invention developed for military use, plays an important part in aviation and weather forecasting today.

Gatling gun

Maxim gun

Machine guns were developed in the 1800's, but inventors of the 1500's experimented with a weapon that had several guns bound together or spread out in a row. A device fitted to the gun barrels made them all fire at once. The Gatling gun of 1862 had several barrels spun by turning a handle. In 1883, American-born inventor Hiram Maxim made the first fully automatic machine gun.

The first aerial bombs were hung from hot-air balloons flown above Venice, Italy, by the Austrian Army in 1849. The bombs had slow-burning fuses but most exploded in the air, causing little damage.

Edward Jenner was the pioneer of vaccination.

The thousands of inventions and discoveries brought about by social needs have eased health threats and helped people live longer. Many such discoveries have made our lives easier and more comfortable.

Through the microscope

Before the 1500's, doctors had little real idea of what caused disease. Then about 1590, a Dutch spectacle-maker called Zacharias Janssen made the first compound microscope. He used glass lenses, like those used for making eyeglasses, which had been available since the late 1200's.

With the microscope, scientists could study the human body in detail. In the mid-1670's, a Dutchman named Anton van Leeuwenhoek used his microscope to study organisms invisible to the unaided eye. He discovered the microscopic organisms that are now called bacteria. Leeuwenhoek did not understand what these strange organisms were, but his studies paved the way for the eventual discovery that certain germs or microbes cause disease.

The first vaccination

In the 1700's, people dreaded catching the common disease called smallpox, which could kill or leave terrible scars. However, some victims recovered from the disease, and doctors had known for hundreds of years that these people never caught smallpox again. They had developed lifelong immunity (resistance) to it. In 1796, an English doctor called Edward Jenner discovered a safe method of making people immune to smallpox.

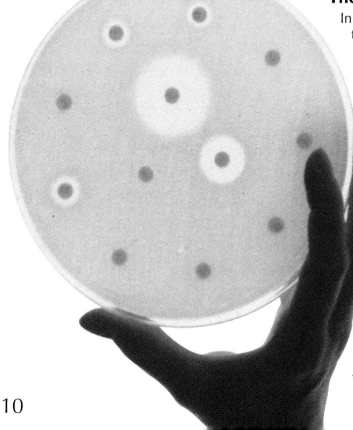

Antibiotics are now used to kill harmful bacteria. The dark circles in this picture are different antibiotics being tested. The surrounding light areas show where the bacteria have been killed.

Edward Jenner risked his reputation as a doctor when he gave the first vaccination for smallpox to James Phipps in England in 1796.

Many people believed that dairymaids who caught cowpox – a relatively harmless disease that caused sores on the hands – could not catch smallpox. Jenner took matter from a dairymaid's cowpox sore and inserted it into a cut made on the arm of a healthy boy. The boy developed cowpox. But when Jenner later inoculated the boy with matter from a smallpox sore, the boy did not develop the disease. His body had built up an immunity to smallpox. Jenner's experiment showed that vaccination worked.

Inventions in the home

Look at the many appliances and products we now have in our homes to make life easier and more comfortable. Most have appeared since the late 1800's, when electric power became available. The vacuum cleaner, first manufactured around 1900, was just one of many devices that reduced housework. Refrigeration helped keep food fresh and brought convenience foods to the kitchen. Electronic devices, such as calculators, are now taken for granted.

A handheld calculator.

Ice was the only way to refrigerate food at home before the 1920's, when mechanical refrigerators were introduced. Several times a week, blocks of ice were delivered to people's homes for use in their icebox.

Chilled and frozen foods are displayed in supermarket refrigerators. Refrigeration keeps foods at temperatures near or below freezing. Low temperatures slow down or stop the growth of microorganisms that spoil food, and so food keeps fresh longer.

How People Invent

Cuneiform writing consists of wedge-shaped characters stamped on clay. This clay cylinder was inscribed in Babylon during the 500's B.C.

Smoke signals were an early form of long-distance communication. Prehistoric people saw the need for such communication, but lacked the knowledge and technical know-how to invent the radio or the telephone.

Before the 1900's, most inventions were made by people who worked alone, using their personal knowledge and skills. Today, the individual inventor has largely been replaced by teams of scientists and technicians working in laboratories.

Need and knowledge

A successful inventor must answer a need, but this is easier said than done. Although prehistoric people saw the need for sending messages quickly, they could not build a radio set. Instead they had to rely on signals, such as smoke from a fire, and send only limited information – a warning, for example.

To create an invention, the inventor must have some practical understanding of how it will work. The bow and arrow, for example, was one of the earliest and most important inventions. The person who made the first bow had to know that a tree branch could bend. The same inventor also had to understand that an arrow could be shot by pulling back and then releasing a string attached to both ends of the branch. To do this, the inventor had to study tree branches and experiment with branches and strings. He or she could then make the first bow and arrow.

Egyptian	Semitic	Phoenician	Greek	Roman	Modern
About 3000 B.C.	About 1500 B.C.	About 1000 B.C.	About 600 B.C.	A.D. 114	
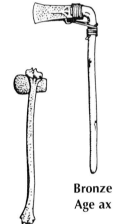					

The letters of the alphabet have developed over many centuries. This illustration shows how the letter A came to have its familiar appearance.

Passing on knowledge

From about 8000 B.C. to 3000 B.C., more and more people began farming instead of hunting and gathering. This new way of life brought a great increase in human knowledge and skills. At first, knowledge of these new skills was passed on by word of mouth. Then, about 5,500 years ago, the Sumerians who lived in what is now Iraq developed the first known system of writing. Now people could write down their knowledge and pass it on to future generations.

People learned to make better tools. A bronze ax was sharper and lasted longer than a stone ax.

Bronze Age ax

Stone Age ax

2050 to 1900 B.C.	1900 to 1000 B.C.	1000 to 150 B.C.

Pottery was first made about 13,000 years ago. Different shapes and ways of making pottery developed. These clay pots were made in Mexico.

Stone Age people gradually improved their toolmaking methods. Two people worked together to split bladelike slivers from a large stone. In this way, they could make several flint tools from one stone.

The alchemist's workshop was the forerunner of the modern chemical laboratory. Alchemists used such laboratory equipment as funnels, strainers, and balance scales.

An iron foundry painted in 1871 by John Ferguson Weir. New technologies made it possible to make iron and steel more cheaply and in larger quantities.

An inventor must have the technical skill to create a working model from an original idea, as well as the necessary materials, parts, and tools.

Alchemists' magic

Alchemy is a blend of science, magic, and mystical ideas that was popular from the early centuries A.D. until the 1700's. Alchemists tried to turn other metals into gold, and to find the elixir of life – a magic potion that would cure disease and lengthen life. They failed in these aims, but by preparing and studying chemical substances, they gained knowledge. The alchemists' experiments helped develop the science of chemistry.

New ways from old

Metalworking techniques also developed over many hundreds of years after early peoples learned how to heat, mix, and shape metals. From these ancient methods, metalworkers developed new and better ways of production in the 1800's. New foundries made iron and steel to build new machines, such as railroad locomotives.

Horse-drawn coaches were the chief means of transportation before railroads were developed.

GOING UP!

The first elevator with a safety device was demonstrated by Elisha G. Otis of New York in 1854.

- The ancient Greek mathematician Archimedes invented a type of elevator powered by ropes and pulleys before 230 B.C. It could carry one person.

- By the 1840's, hydraulic and steam-powered elevators were in use. Hydraulic elevators were very slow, and the ropes of steam elevators often broke.

- Otis invented a safety device that prevented an elevator from falling if the ropes broke.

- The world's first all-passenger elevator was installed in New York City in 1857.

- The first electric elevator started operating in 1889.

Inventing the railroad

There were railroads before the 1800's, but the wagons used on such railroads were pulled by horses. No engine yet existed that could do the work better than a horse. Inventors built the first steam engines in the 1600's, to pump water out of flooded mines. Later, improved steam engines were developed to power factory machines, and in the late 1700's, inventors began trying to use steam engines to power vehicles. They made steam-engined vehicles that could run on iron rails and pull heavier loads than teams of horses could. People too were keen to travel in this novel way, and in the early 1800's, steam trains became a familiar sight. Railroad builders used new tools and skills to construct the tracks and the locomotives that pulled the first trains. A new industry had been created.

The world's first public steam railroad opened in northern England on September 27, 1825. George Stephenson's engine *Locomotion No. 1* pulled the first train.

Glider flights made by Orville and Wilbur Wright helped them solve many problems of flight control (left, below). They worked in secret, before making the world's first airplane flight in December 1903 (left).

Many good ideas have come only after a long period of trial and error. "Try and try again" is a good motto for an inventor! But, once in a while, an inventor gets an idea as a result of an accident.

Creative insight

It may take years of patient work for an inventor to arrive at the key idea that blends imagination, knowledge, and technical capacity into an invention. Or it may come as a flash of inspiration.

Trial and error

When they were trying to build a flying machine, Orville and Wilbur Wright knew they needed a wing shape that would help lift the machine off the ground. The brothers tried many shapes before finding the right one.

Keeping going

In 1919, the American rocket pioneer Robert H. Goddard published a report describing the kind of rocket flight necessary to reach the moon. When newspapers made fun of his ideas, Goddard avoided further publicity, but kept working on his research. In 1926, he succeeded in launching a small rocket – the forerunner of our space rockets today.

The evolution of an idea

Charles Darwin got the information that led to his ideas about evolution during a voyage around the world between 1831 and 1836. Everywhere he went, he studied plants and animals. On the Galapagos Islands in the Pacific Ocean, he noticed many variations among plants and animals of the same general type as those he had seen in South America. This set him thinking. Why were they different? On his return to England, he spent many years studying the notes and specimens he had brought back. Finally he published his revolutionary ideas on the evolution of species.

The first successful liquid-propellant rocket was launched in 1926 by Robert H. Goddard.

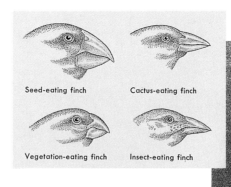

Seed-eating finch   Cactus-eating finch

Vegetation-eating finch   Insect-eating finch

Charles Darwin, a British naturalist, published his theory of evolution in 1859 in a famous book called *The Origin of Species.* In South America, Darwin had found fossils of extinct animals that closely resembled living species. He also saw different kinds of finches. Over many generations, these birds had developed different shaped beaks adapted to eat various kinds of food, and the different groups had evolved into separate species. Darwin's ideas revolutionized thinking about biology.

An accidental discovery

For five years the American inventor Charles Goodyear tried to find some way of making rubber a more useful product. He wanted rubber that would not melt in the heat or become brittle and stiff in the cold. One winter night in 1839, he was at home talking to his brother when he accidentally dropped a piece of rubber that he had sprinkled with sulfur onto a red-hot stove. Instead of melting, the rubber flattened out into a small disk. It still felt flexible and strong. Goodyear hung the disk on his doorpost overnight in the winter cold. Next morning, it was still rubber-like. Goodyear had discovered vulcanization, a process that gives rubber elasticity, hardness, and strength.

The bicycle was developed from the draisienne (above), invented about 1817 by Baron Karl von Drais of Germany. It had no pedals and was pushed along by the rider's feet. In 1839 a Scottish blacksmith, Kirkpatrick Macmillan made the first bicycle, adding pedals to the draisienne.

Charles Goodyear discovered vulcanization in 1839, after years of unsuccessful experiments with rubber. In the end, his invention was the result of an accident.

Pneumatic tires were developed by John Dunlop of Great Britain in 1888. He first made the air-filled rubber tires to provide a smoother ride for his son's tricycle.

The safety bicycle had been invented by 1885, complete with handlebars, and pedals driving a chain linked to the back wheel.

Researchers may aim at a practical goal, such as creating a new product or improving an existing one. This car-crash test helps in the development of safer vehicles.

In today's world, an inventor working alone is rare. No individual inventor could acquire all the scientific and technical knowledge available in a modern research laboratory.

In the laboratory

The transistor is one of the most important electronic devices ever developed. Its invention is an example of how research laboratories work. In the late 1930's, the Bell System operated most of the telephones in the United States. The company expected a growth in telephone usage, and asked its research organization – Bell Telephone Laboratories – to find a way to handle the increase. Scientists and engineers decided they needed to create a device that would improve the way telephone-switching equipment worked. This equipment controls the number of calls that can be placed at one time. The new device would need to be more powerful.

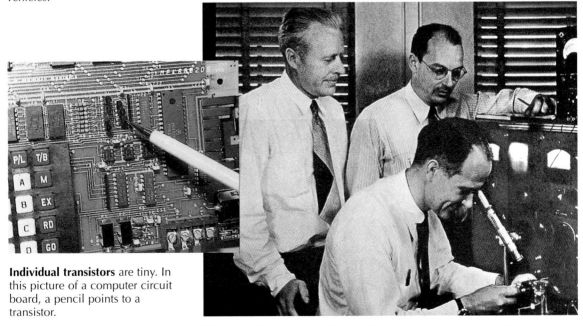

Individual transistors are tiny. In this picture of a computer circuit board, a pencil points to a transistor.

The team that invented the transistor consisted of the American physicists William Shockley (seated), Walter Brattain (left), and John Bardeen (right).

A one-man research team

The American statesman Benjamin Franklin (1706-1790) was a remarkable person, a jack-of-all-trades and master of many. He flew a kite into a thunderstorm to show that lightning is electricity. (This was a very dangerous experiment!) His lightning rod saved many buildings from fires caused by lightning. He invented bifocal glasses for distance and reading use. And he invented an improved stove that used less fuel than other stoves and gave more heat.

Franklin and his kite

Franklin's glasses

The Franklin stove

The lightning rod

A vital part of the switching equipment was the vacuum tube. The inventors decided to try to create a device more efficient than this tube. Scientists and engineers shared their knowledge of mathematics, physics, and materials, and by 1947 they had come up with a new device – the transistor. The transistor is lighter, smaller, and longer-lasting than the vacuum tube. It also uses less power.

Scientists work in laboratories. In this biochemical laboratory, scientists observe specimens under a microscope. The researcher on the left is working at a fume cupboard. The cupboard has an extraction system to prevent poisons and germs from entering the laboratory atmosphere.

Edison at age 14.

Thomas Edison, the great American inventor, began his researches when he was 12. His baggagecar laboratory, shown in this restoration, was part of the train on which he worked.

Early Inventions

From earliest times, people have been curious about the world around them. The first inventions appeared many thousands of years ago, during the Stone Age.

The cultivation of a date palm is shown in this carving from ancient Mesopotamia. The first farmers added much to people's knowledge of plants and animals.

Stone Age inventors

The Old Stone Age lasted from about 2.5 million years ago to about 8000 B.C. During this time, people learned how to make axes and other tools by chipping bone, flint, horn, ivory, and stones into the shapes they wanted. They also invented the bow and arrow and the spear.

Later, when people learned how to grow crops, they settled in villages, from which grew the first cities. Over time, people developed new skills such as pottery-making and textile-weaving.

Metals and the wheel

No one knows when people first made objects from metal. By 3500 B.C., people had learned that tin and copper could be melted to make bronze. Bronze was stronger and lasted longer than either tin or copper.

About the same time, the wheel – one of the most important inventions in history – was invented. Before they had the wheel, people carried burdens on their backs or dragged them on heavy sleds. The invention of the wheel led to the development of wagons, which enabled people to move goods more easily and over longer distances.

Egyptian metalworkers are shown in this wall painting from about 1474 B.C. Some workers are heating rocks to extract the metal that the rocks contain, while others pour hot, liquid metal into molds.

Early wheels, as on this oxcart, were made from pieces of solid wood.

An irrigation device called a shadoof was used by the ancient Egyptians to draw water from the Nile River for their crops.

The first civilizations

The first civilizations developed between about 3500 and 3100 B.C. in the Nile Valley of Egypt and between the Tigris and Euphrates rivers of Mesopotamia (modern Iraq). The first civilizations were based on agriculture, and farmland was fertile in these river valleys. The people of the first civilizations developed new skills, including writing and mathematics. The Egyptians used geometry to build the huge pyramids. As early as 3000 B.C., they studied the sky to forecast the seasons and to predict the annual flooding of the Nile River.

A great civilization developed in Greece by about the 500's B.C. The ancient Greeks are best known for their achievements in the arts, philosophy, and science. They also made many inventions.

Archimedes (left) was a Greek mathematician and inventor whose Archimedean screw (below) was used as an irrigation device. He also studied levers and pulleys, and made the remark, "Give me a place to stand on, and I will move the entire earth."

Three Greek inventors

- **Ctesibius was a Greek inventor who lived during the 200's B.C. in Alexandria, Egypt. He built the first water pump.**

- **Archimedes lived during the 200's B.C. in Syracuse. He invented the Archimedean screw to raise water from a lower level to a higher one. He also invented cranes for pulling enemy warships out of the water and twirling them around.**

- **Hero lived in Alexandria during the first century A.D. He invented a screw press for squeezing juice from grapes or olives. He also invented a simple steam turbine – as an amusing toy.**

The Spread of Knowledge

A pottery jar made in China about 1200 B.C.

During the period from the A.D. 400's to the 1500's, life changed in Europe and in Asia. Many of these changes resulted from inventions in agriculture, transportation, and warfare. Knowledge of ancient inventions also spread.

Chinese inventions

Many important inventions were made in ancient China and in time some of these inventions reached Europe. The Chinese invented paper more than 2,000 years ago, and made the world's first porcelain. The Chinese also invented the magnetic compass, which helped sailors crossing oceans navigate accurately when they could not use the stars or sun as guides.

Easier on horse and rider

The invention of the rigid horse collar about A.D. 800 made farming easier and helped overland travel. Before this invention, horses wore a throat harness that cut off their breathing when they pulled too hard. The rigid collar shifted the pressure of the load to the horse's shoulders, enabling the animal to pull a much heavier load.

The magnetic compass (below) was invented in China about A.D. 1100. The first known magnets were lodestones, rocks that contain a natural mineral called magnetite.

Wonders of China

Westerners such as Marco Polo, who visited China in the 1200's, were amazed at the wonders they saw. The Chinese people produced many of the world's most important inventions.

- The Chinese were the first to make silk, using silkworms. No one in the West saw the mysterious worm (actually a caterpillar) until about A.D. 550.

- Chinese ships were the first to use sternpost rudders, in about 1300. Before this invention, ships were steered near the stern by large, awkward oars that often broke during storms.

- The Chinese made glazed pottery as early as the 1300's B.C. Porcelain, a type of ceramic valued for its beauty and strength, was another Chinese invention and came to be known as china.

- The Chinese used the wheelbarrow in the A.D. 300's. This simple but useful load-carrier did not appear in Europe until the 1200's.

Wheelbarrows were used in China to carry passengers as well as loads.

Riding a horse was aided by the use of the stirrup, an invention that came to Europe from India by way of China. The stirrup, when added to a saddle, helped soldiers to fight on horseback with less risk of slipping off the horse.

Studying the heavens

Chinese astronomers had charted the positions of the stars by the 1300's B.C., and recorded eclipses of the sun and moon. Pythagoras, a Greek who lived during the 500's B.C., argued that the earth is round. Greek astronomers worked out systems to explain the motion of the planets. Most explained – wrongly – that the planets, the sun and moon, and the stars revolved around the earth. But during the 200's B.C., Aristarchus of Samos suggested – rightly – that all the planets, including the earth, revolve around the sun. However, this idea was not accepted until the 1500's, and most people continued to believe that the earth was the center of the universe.

Horses wearing collars were more useful as working animals. This picture from the 1500's shows farm horses at work.

Arab astronomers of the A.D. 800's and 900's mapped the stars in the night sky.

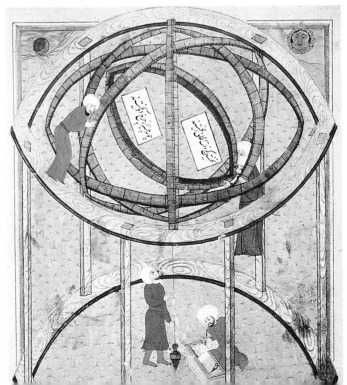

A recipe for cough syrup made from plants appears in an Arabic manuscript from the 1220's. The Arabs made important contributions to plant science and medicine.

The Age of Ideas

A time of new ideas and exploration flourished in Europe from about 1300 to 1600. This period was called the Renaissance – a Latin term meaning "rebirth." During the Renaissance, artists and scholars studied the learning and art of ancient Greece and Rome. Their new-found knowledge was spread by one of history's most important inventions – printing.

Printing from movable type was invented in Asia during the 1000's and in Europe during the 1400's. This picture shows a printing shop of the 1600's. On the left, typesetters assemble blocks of letters or type to form pages. In the background, an assistant inks a page. On the right, a printer turns a huge screw on the printing press to push paper against the inked type.

The printing press

Printing with movable type is an example of how a new invention can be created from several inventions that already exist. Movable type (letters made from wood or metal), ink, paper, and the screw press had all been invented long before the 1400's. Johannes Gutenberg of Germany used all these inventions in the mid-1400's to produce printing. Before Gutenberg, books were written and copied by hand. Printed books were much quicker and cheaper to make. Gutenberg's invention put more knowledge into the hands of more people at less cost than ever before. It became the first means of mass communication.

This flying machine was drawn about 1500 by Leonardo da Vinci. He sketched a machine with flapping wings, but it never flew. In Leonardo's time, the engine that could power a flying machine had not yet been invented.

Leonardo's notes

Leonardo recorded his ideas about art, engineering, and science in notebooks.

- About 4,200 pages of these notebooks still exist.

- They include sketches of machines, and the first accurate drawings of the human body.

- Leonardo wrote his notes backward, so they can be read only if the page is held up to a mirror.

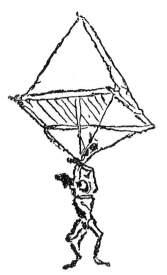

Leonardo da Vinci

Leonardo, one of the most versatile geniuses in history, was born in 1452 near Florence, Italy. He became one of the world's greatest painters, but he also studied the human body, astronomy, plants, and rocks. He designed machines and drew plans for hundreds of inventions. Many of his ideas were far ahead of his time. For example, he drew plans for a flying machine and a parachute.

A parachute was drawn by Leonardo da Vinci in 1495.

Bodies and blood

The first scientific studies of the human body were made in the 1500's by Andreas Vesalius, a professor of medicine at the University of Padua in Italy. Vesalius examined corpses to learn more about how the human body worked. He wrote the first scientific textbook on human anatomy in 1543.

In the early 1600's, the English physician William Harvey discovered how blood circulates through the body. He found that the heart pumps blood through the arteries to all parts of the body, and that the blood returns to the heart through the veins. Harvey's work marked a turning point in medical history.

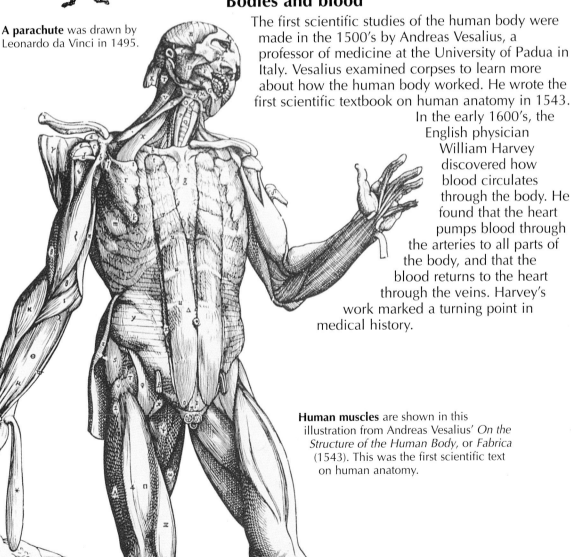

Human muscles are shown in this illustration from Andreas Vesalius' *On the Structure of the Human Body*, or *Fabrica* (1543). This was the first scientific text on human anatomy.

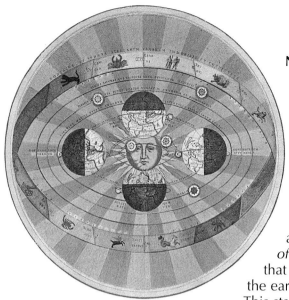

The system of the universe proposed by Copernicus in 1543 placed the sun, not the earth, at the center.

New discoveries began to challenge old ideas. Astronomers realized that the earth was not, after all, the center of the universe.

The sun and the planets

During the Renaissance, scholars began to challenge ideas that had been held for centuries. For example, most people believed that the earth was the center of the universe. Then in 1543, the Polish astronomer Nicolaus Copernicus put forward a new theory in his book *On the Revolutions of the Heavenly Spheres.* Copernicus suggested that the sun is the center of the universe, and that the earth and the other planets move around the sun. This startling idea was followed by new discoveries. In the late 1500's, the Danish astronomer Tycho Brahe observed the movement of the planets far more precisely than ever before. Then Brahe's assistant, Johannes Kepler of Germany, discovered that the planets travel round the sun in an oval-shaped path, or ellipse. Copernicus had thought that the planets moved around the sun in circles.

Galileo's cannon balls

If you dropped a heavy stone and a light stone from the same height, which one would hit the ground first? Galileo wanted to prove the answer.

According to a famous story, Galileo climbed to the top of the Leaning Tower of Pisa. He then dropped two cannon balls, one heavy and one lighter, at the same instant. The two balls hit the ground at nearly the same time. This story may not be true, but Galileo's reasoning – that all bodies fall at the same rate and that the slight time difference taken for the balls to hit the ground was caused by air resistance – was correct.

The matter was settled after the air pump was invented about 1650. If the air was pumped out of a long tube, a vacuum was created inside. Then a feather and a coin dropped down the tube at the same instant would fall side by side and reach the bottom together.

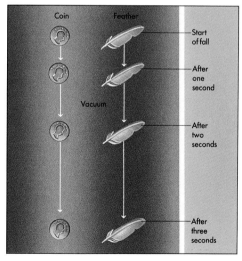

Bodies falling freely in a vacuum descend at the same speed, regardless of their size, shape, and weight – as shown in this diagram. Galileo guessed this, though he was never able to carry out the experiment in a vacuum.

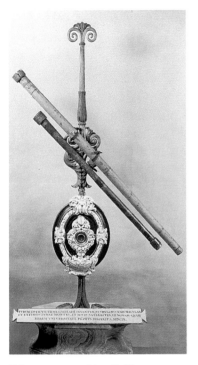

Telescopes used by Galileo.

Galileo finds the moon's mountains

The first person to use a telescope to study the sky was Galileo Galilei (1564-1642), an Italian astronomer and physicist and one of the world's greatest scientists. The telescope was probably first made by a Dutch optician named Hans Lippershey in 1608, when he mounted two glass lenses in a narrow tube. News of the invention spread quickly.

Within a year, Galileo had made his own telescope and turned it to the stars. There he saw four moons revolving around the planet Jupiter. According to the old ideas – accepted since the time of the ancient Greeks – all the stars and planets and moons revolved around the earth. Now this was seen to be untrue. The new invention helped prove that Copernicus had been right.

Galileo also looked at the moon through his telescope. He discovered that, far from being perfectly smooth as the ancient Greeks had thought, the moon had a rough surface with mountains and craters.

Galileo built his own telescopes to study the sky. New scientific devices such as the telescope brought a rapid growth of knowledge in the 1600's and 1700's.

A pendulum clock made in 1641 was designed by Galileo, who saw the need for precise scientific instruments.

Newton and a New World

By the 1600's, scientific activity and knowledge was rapidly increasing. One of the foremost scientists of the time was Isaac Newton.

A painting of Isaac Newton made by an unknown artist about 1726, a year before the great scientist died.

The young scientist

Newton was born in Lincolnshire, England, in 1642. As a boy, he enjoyed making machines more than studying. He invented a small windmill for grinding wheat, a water clock, and a sundial. Newton became a student at Cambridge University, though he showed no particular promise. However, in just 18 months between 1665 and 1667, Isaac Newton made discoveries which changed the way we see the world.

What stops the universe from falling apart?

Newton left Cambridge during an outbreak of plague and went to live in the country. During this time, he suddenly realized that the same force that pulls an object to earth also keeps the moon in its orbit. This force of *universal gravitation* makes bodies in the universe attract each other. Newton proved that many types of motion are due to that one kind of force. He showed that the gravitational force of the sun keeps the planets in their orbits.

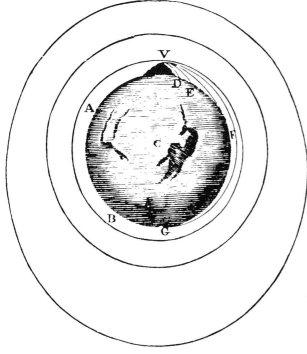

A diagram by Newton shows what happens to an object that is launched from a great height and at different speeds around the earth. His work explains why the moon orbits the earth, and why we can launch satellites that travel around our planet.

Newton and the apple

When Newton was 23, the sight of an apple falling from a tree caused him to question how far the force of gravity reaches. He realized that the same force that pulled the apple from the tree holds the moon in its orbit around the earth. One version of this story says the apple hit Newton on the head as he sat beneath the tree!

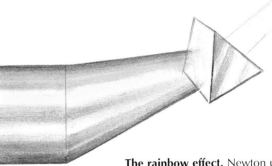

The rainbow effect. Newton used a glass prism to show that white light is made up of all colors, forming a band like a rainbow.

Newton's other discoveries

Newton also discovered the secrets of light and color. And he invented a branch of mathematics called *calculus*, which was also devised independently by Gottfried Leibniz, a German mathematician.

The world hears of Newton's work

Although Newton finished his first investigations on gravity and motion by 1666, nothing more was heard of them for nearly 20 years. Meanwhile, he continued to teach mathematics at Cambridge, where he was a professor.

Then one day, astronomer Edmond Halley, scientist Robert Hooke, and architect Christopher Wren were discussing the force that makes the planets move around the sun. What is it? The three men could not solve this problem. Halley went to see Newton, and found that the Cambridge professor had a complete proof of the law of gravity. Halley persuaded Newton to publish his findings, and they appeared in 1687 in *Philosophiae Naturalis Principia Mathematica (Mathematical Principles of Natural Philosophy)*. This book was the first to present a unified system of scientific principles explaining what happens on earth and in the heavens. Modern physics would not have been possible without Newton's discoveries.

This reflecting telescope was designed by Newton. It used a reflecting mirror instead of the glass lenses of earlier refracting telescopes.

The Industrial Revolution

The 1700's and early 1800's were times of rapid change for the people of Europe and North America. Their ways of life and the type of work they did were greatly affected by industrialization, especially by the invention of new machines such as the steam engine.

Large ironworks made Britain the world's leading iron producer during the Industrial Revolution.

Steam for pumps

The Industrial Revolution – as this period of change is called – began in Great Britain, a country which had plenty of coal and iron ore, the two natural resources on which early industrialization depended. The driving force of industrialization was the steam engine, developed by James Watt. Watt was a Scottish inventor but the steam engine was not his invention. The first practical steam engine was designed in 1698 by an Englishman named Thomas Savery. It was used as a pump to drain water from mines.

In 1712, Thomas Newcomen, an English tool seller, invented a steam-engine pump with a large beam balanced across the middle like a seesaw. A piston inside a cylinder hung from one end of the beam. When steam entered the cylinder, it forced the piston up, lowering the other end of the beam. Cold water was then sprayed into the cylinder, and the steam condensed (cooled and turned to water).

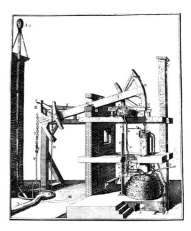

Thomas Newcomen's steam engine drove a pump to remove water from mines. This machine was bulky and wasteful of fuel. It turned only a fraction of the energy it received into useful work.

Using iron

- Prehistoric people made tools from lumps of iron they found in meteorites that had fallen to earth from space. In several early languages, the word for *iron* meant "metal from the sky."

- By about 1400 B.C., the Hittites, who lived in what is now Turkey, had learned to make iron from rocks containing iron ore.

- From the A.D. 400's to the 1500's, ironworkers produced iron by heating iron ore and charcoal in brick-lined shaft furnaces.

- During the 1700's, ironmakers in Britain began to use coke instead of charcoal in their furnaces.

This left a vacuum inside the cylinder which sucked the piston down again and so raised the other end of the beam, which was attached to the piston of a pump in a mine.

Watt's engines

The Newcomen engine used a great deal of steam, so it burned a lot of wood or coal as fuel. In 1763, somebody asked James Watt to repair a model of a Newcomen steam engine. Watt, a maker of mathematical instruments, saw that first heating, and then cooling, the cylinder wasted heat. Watt then invented a better engine, in which the condenser and the cylinder were separate. The cylinder remained hot. This new arrangement used only one-fourth of the fuel of an older Newcomen engine.

More power

Watt continued to improve the steam engine. For example, he built engines in which the steam was used first on one side of the piston, then on the other. And Watt's engines could do a variety of tasks other than pumping. A linking mechanism changed the up-and-down motion of the engine into rotary, or round-and-round, motion. The improved Watt engines could now drive other machines.

James Watt never used high-pressure steam because he feared an explosion. By the early 1800's, other inventors – including Richard Trevithick of Britain and Oliver Evans of the United States – had built engines that used steam at high pressure, and so produced greater power.

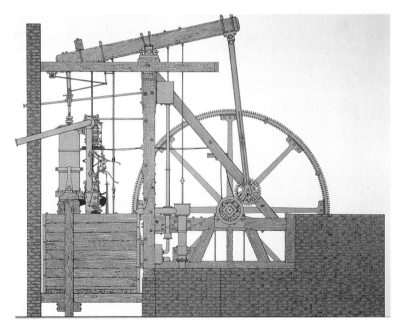

James Watt's steam engine, developed in the late 1700's, led to the widespread use of steam power in industry.

Factories

Most of the goods we buy today are made in factories. Factory manufacturing was made possible in the late 1700's and 1800's by the invention of new machines and processes.

By the early 1900's, cars were being built on assembly lines in the United States. In 1914, this assembly line was used to manufacture Ford Model T cars in Michigan.

Robots weld cars in a modern factory where electricity provides the power for many machines, including the computers that control the robots.

Steam for all uses

Other inventors found new uses for Watt's steam engine. In 1787, John Fitch of the United States demonstrated the first workable steamboat. In Britain, Richard Trevithick invented the steam locomotive in 1804, and in 1839 a Scottish engineer, James Nasmyth, made the first steam hammer.

Machine tools

When Watt began to experiment with the steam engine, he could not find a tool that drilled a perfectly round hole. As a result, his engines leaked steam. In 1775, an English ironmaker named John Wilkinson invented a new boring machine that drilled a more precise hole. Other inventors designed a planing tool that smoothed the surfaces of the steam engine's metal parts.

Without the development of these machine tools, the enormous potential of the steam engine and power-driven machinery could not have been achieved.

The spinning jenny invented by James Hargreaves was operated by a large wheel. Women were employed to work the new machines.

Samuel Crompton's first spinning mule was operated by hand, but later versions of this machine were driven by water power.

Textile machinery

In the 1760's two machines revolutionized the textile industry. First came the spinning jenny, invented by James Hargreaves, an English weaver and carpenter, in 1764. The other important new machine was the water frame, invented in 1769 by another Englishman, Richard Arkwright.

A machine that combined features of both the spinning jenny and the water frame was developed in Britain between 1774 and 1779 by a weaver named Samuel Crompton. It was known as the spinning mule and, in time, it replaced both the earlier machines. The spinning mule ended the home spinning industry. However, weaving was still done on handlooms, until the mid-1780's when an English clergyman named Edmund Cartwright developed a steam-powered loom. Soon weaving too had become a factory process.

Mass production

Other countries followed Britain in industrializing. They included Belgium, France, Germany, and the United States. By the end of the 1800's, factory owners were looking for ever more efficient ways of making goods, using machines.

Take the automobile, for example. Before 1900, skilled craftworkers made cars one at a time – in the way they had built wagons. However, mass-production methods had been used since the mid-1800's to produce firearms and farm equipment. To build vehicles faster, the same methods were applied to carmaking.

In 1901 in the United States, Ransom E. Olds began to mass-produce cars from parts sent in to his factory by outside suppliers. In 1913, Henry Ford installed a moving assembly line in his car factory. The frame of a car was pulled through the plant by a chain. Workers stood on each side, and assembled the car by adding parts brought to them on moving conveyor belts. The system saved time and money. The factory revolution had moved on.

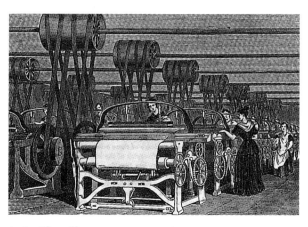

In textile mills, women operated looms powered by steam engines or water wheels.

Machines on the Farm

New machines changed farm life in the 1800's. Machines like McCormick's reaper were the forerunners of modern combines.

McCormick's reaper

Cyrus McCormick was born in 1809 on a farm in Virginia. He experimented with machinery to make farming easier, and watched his father try, without success, to build a machine that would harvest grain. At harvest time farmers still cut their crops with hand scythes – cutting tools that had changed little in thousands of years.

In 1831 Cyrus built his first reaper. This machine had a straight cutting blade linked by gears to a drive wheel. As the wheel turned, the blade moved back and forth and sawed through the stalks of grain. Projecting rods caught and held the stalks while the blade cut through them. The stalks fell onto a platform and a worker raked them onto the ground. Several other workers bound the sheaves. The machine sold well and McCormick gained worldwide fame.

The first seed drill or planter was invented by Jethro Tull of England about 1700. Before this, farmers scattered seeds by hand.

The first successful harvesting machine was the reaper invented by Cyrus McCormick.

An early gasoline-driven tractor did only light work, but it marked the start of a new age of power for agriculture. Farmers no longer needed horses to pull plows and other machinery. They needed fewer workers too.

The sulky plow was pulled by horses, while the farmer rode.

The Plow

- About 8,000 years ago, an unknown farmer sharpened one prong of a forked branch to turn the soil. The plow had been invented.

- The walking plow was pulled by oxen, horses, or mules. The farmer walked behind to steer the plow.

- The sulky plow was invented by John Deere, an Illinois blacksmith, in 1875. Now the farmer could ride while he worked.

- The steam-powered plows that appeared in the early 1900's were less efficient than the tractor plows farmers use today.

Later inventors worked to improve the reaper so that fewer workers would be needed. In the 1870's, the American inventor Sylvanus D. Locke produced a binder that bound the sheaves and dropped them on the ground. By the 1920's many farmers used tractors to pull binders. Since then, reapers have been replaced by combined harvester-threshers, or combines.

An early threshing machine was powered by horses walking on a treadmill. Threshing removed grain from the stalks of cereal crops.

Steam on Rails, Steam at Sea

The invention of the steam engine started the greatest revolution in transportation since the invention of the wheel and the sailing ship.

Early steamships had sails as well as steam engines, in case the engines broke down. This steamship of the 1800's was driven by paddlewheels.

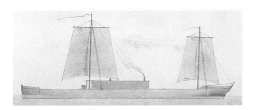

The *Clermont*, built by Robert Fulton, was the first steamboat to carry paying passengers. Its first successful voyage was a trip up the Hudson River. Fulton made this watercolor sketch of the steamboat in 1808.

Fulton's steamboat

The American steamboat pioneer Robert Fulton was born on a farm in Pennsylvania in 1765. As a boy, he made household utensils for his mother, and skyrockets for a town celebration. He became a painter and went to England to study art, but he was more interested in inventing. He designed canal boats, and a machine for digging canals.

In 1801, Fulton built a submarine called the *Nautilus*, which was able to dive and surface. His ideas about underwater craft interested both the French and British governments, but neither adopted them wholeheartedly. In 1803, Fulton learned that a steam-engined boat had been tested on the Seine River in Paris. Fulton ordered one of James Watt's steam engines and returned to the United States, where he constructed his own steamboat.

Up the river

This craft was registered as the *North River Steamboat* but was generally called the *Clermont*. It steamed from New York City to Albany in 1807, and soon it was providing regular passenger service on the Hudson River. In 1819, the American ship *Savannah* became the first steam-powered vessel to cross the Atlantic Ocean. However, it used sails for most of the 29-day trip.

Railroads began carrying freight and passengers during the 1830's. On some railroads, horses as well as steam locomotives were used to pull wagons.

The first locomotive was a simple steam engine built by Richard Trevithick in 1804.

**The *Rocket*, the first truly successful railroad locomotive, was built in England in 1829 by George Stephenson.

An early steam locomotive built by Richard Trevithick attracted curious Londoners in 1808.

Steam on the rails

The first steam railroad to run regular freight services began in Britain in 1825, and a passenger railroad opened in 1830. The locomotives hauling the trains were built by George Stephenson, a British engineer. The pioneer work on steam railroads had been done earlier by Richard Trevithick.

Trevithick was a mining engineer, born in Cornwall, England, in 1771. He built high-pressure steam engines to pump water from the local tin mines, and then turned to making a machine that would run under its own power.

Pulling power

In 1801 Trevithick built a steam carriage that ran on the road. In 1804 he built the first steam locomotive to run on rails. It pulled a load of iron along a railroad made for horse-drawn trucks.

Trevithick's locomotives were too heavy for the roads and railroads of his time. Other inventors, such as Stephenson, made the puffing, hissing locomotive the wonder of its age.

STEAMBOAT FIRSTS

- In 1783, the Marquis Claude de Jouffroy d'Abbans, a French nobleman, built a steamboat that made a 15-minute river trip.

- In 1787, John Fitch, an American inventor, made the first workable steamboat in the United States. Its engine powered a series of paddles on each side of the boat. Fitch started a passenger service in 1790, but lacked the money to keep operating.

- In 1802, William Symington, a British engineer, built a steam tug that had a paddlewheel at the stern. It worked perfectly, but Symington also ran out of money.

- In 1809, the *Phoenix* became the first steamboat to make an ocean voyage as it chugged from New York City to Philadelphia. This steamboat was built by John Stevens, an American engineer.

- In 1838, the British steamer *Sirius* became the first ship to offer regular scheduled service across the Atlantic Ocean under steam power alone.

Steam locomotives could pull heavier trains faster than horses. Soon they were hauling freight and passenger trains and the days of the horse railroads were over.

Steam on the Road

Inventors of the late 1700's dreamed of a "horseless carriage" that could move under its own power. Steam provided the answer.

The Cugnot steam tractor puffed along at less than 2 miles (3 kilometers) per hour.

A false start

Nicholas-Joseph Cugnot, a French army engineer, built two steam vehicles, in 1769 and 1770. One was meant to carry passengers, while the other was a three-wheeled tractor.

Cugnot thought his steam tractor would be better than a team of horses for pulling heavy cannon. Unfortunately, he could not find a safe way to steer the tractor. Nor could he invent a suitable brake. The machine ran out of control and crashed into a wall. His neighbors advised Cugnot to lock the machine away before it killed someone.

This Stanley steam car was built in 1897.

Steaming along

- **For a time, steam cars were as popular as gasoline-engined cars.**

- **In the early 1900's, steam cars set speed records of over 120 miles (193 kilometers) per hour.**

- **The last steam car company in the United States, Stanley Brothers, went bankrupt in 1924.**

Steam carriages

Other steam vehicles were tried, however. In the early 1800's, steam enthusiasts started passenger services on public roads. Rival railroad and stagecoach companies tried to stop the new steam carriages. Steam vehicles were unreliable. They were also very heavy and broke up the surface of dirt roads. They made a terrible noise, hissing steam, puffing out dirty smoke, and frightening horses and pedestrians. Sometimes they exploded.

Follow the flag

In 1865, the British government set speed limits on steam vehicles of 4 miles (6 kilometers) per hour in the country and 2 miles (3 kilometers) per hour in town. To warn of its approach, a signalman had to walk ahead of the vehicle, swinging a red flag by day and a red lantern by night. Not surprisingly, this law put an end to further development of automobiles in Britain for about 30 years. But successful steam cars were built later in several countries, including the United States.

Ambitious amphibian

In 1805, inventor Oliver Evans built what was probably the first self-powered land vehicle in the United States. His machine started off as a steam-driven dredge mounted on a boat. Evans put wheels on his gigantic machine and then drove it through the streets of Philadelphia to the harbor – and into the water.

Steam carriages like this were used on public roads in Britain in the mid-1800's. The body of the carriage was very like that of a horse-drawn stagecoach.

People on Wheels

The discovery of huge oil deposits in Texas in 1901 aided the growth of the car industry by making gasoline more plentiful and cheaper.

The car was invented in the 1880's. A new engine made this modern means of transport possible. Cars, trucks, and buses were soon crowding onto the roads.

The gasoline engine

Several inventors in the 1800's tried to develop an engine that worked better than the steam engine. Jean Joseph Étienne Lenoir, a Belgian living in France, built one of the first practical internal combustion engines in 1860. It produced power by burning fuel inside a closed cylinder. It was simpler, smaller, and more efficient than the steam engine, which burned fuel outside the cylinder. Lenoir's engine burned coke oven gas, and was used to drive machinery, though he also tried it out in a crude motorcar. Other inventors also took up the challenge.

Henry Ford's first car was built in a workshop in Detroit. The car, completed in 1896, is now on display in the Henry Ford Museum in Dearborn, Michigan.

CAR FIRSTS

- In 1885, Gottlieb Daimler and Karl Benz, two Germans working separately, developed the first successful four-stroke gasoline engines.

- In 1891, a French company, Panhard et Levassor, created the basic design of the car as we know it today.

- In 1895, a French rubber-making firm, Michelin, introduced the first automobile tires filled with compressed air.

- In 1896, Henry Ford built his first successful car.

The first automobiles

In the 1880's two German engineers – Gottlieb Daimler and Karl Benz – developed vehicles driven by gasoline engines. Daimler and his partner Wilhelm Maybach made a motor bicycle in 1885 and a four-wheeled car in 1886. Karl Benz drove his first three-wheeled car in 1885. It had electric ignition, a water-cooled engine, and a differential gear – features still common in cars today.

By 1891 the basic design of the car had been fixed. Panhard et Levassor, a French company, placed a Daimler engine in the front of the car and used a revolving chain to transfer power to the rear wheels. Most cars had a front engine and rear-wheel drive until the late 1970's, when front-wheel drive became more popular.

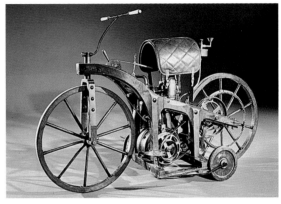

Cats-eyes indicate the road's course to drivers at night. The invention of the car changed the way roads were made. Inventions such as cats-eyes (first used in the 1930's) helped make driving safer. Glass studs reflect the vehicle's headlights. Rubber supports clean the reflecting studs when a vehicle runs over cats-eyes.

The first motorcycle was built in 1885 when German engineer Gottlieb Daimler put a gasoline engine on a bicycle.

Motor vehicles played an important part in World War I (1914-1918). Military trucks like this one moved soldiers and supplies.

Traffic jams became frequent from the 1920's, as a boom in the car industry put more vehicles on the road. This 1922 traffic jam was in New York City.

Dots, Dashes, and Snapshots

Inventors in the 1800's found new ways to transmit words and pictures, making communication faster than ever before.

Words move faster

By 1814, *The Times* newspaper of London was being printed on a new, German-invented steam-driven press. Although the type was still set by hand, the actual printing went hundreds of times faster.

Steamships and locomotives increased the speed at which people and news could travel. Even more rapid communication arrived with the electric telegraph. The first successful telegraph system was developed by Samuel F. B. Morse and his partner, Alfred Vail, using batteries and electromagnets for a stable power source. Telegraph messages were sent in a code of dots and dashes known as Morse code. Newspapers began to use the Morse telegraph at once, and (after an earlier failure) a telegraph cable was laid across the floor of the Atlantic Ocean in 1866.

Morse developed a sounder for the telegraph to click out incoming messages.

In the first public telegraph message, sent from Washington to Baltimore in 1844 and recorded on tape, Morse tapped out the words, "What hath God wrought!"

Home computer

Mobile telephone

A home computer and a mobile telephone are two devices used to speed communications since the 1970's.

Photography

No one person can be called the inventor of photography. The first technique for making photographs – on metal plates exposed to light – was so slow that it could be used only to take pictures of motionless objects. By the 1830's improved techniques, such as the daguerreotype, took only a few minutes. Then William Henry Fox Talbot, a British inventor, began using a paper negative instead of a metal plate. This made it possible to move film through the camera and take a series of pictures, instead of changing the plate after each exposure.

In 1887 an American clergyman named Hannibal W. Goodwin developed a celluloid film that was tough but flexible. George Eastman, who made photographic equipment, introduced the film in 1889, launching the age of the pocket camera and the snapshot. Eastman film was also used in the first movie cameras during the 1890's.

The Kodak camera, invented in 1888 by U.S. manufacturer George Eastman, made picture-taking easy. This photo of Eastman was taken with a Kodak camera like the one he is holding.

In communication

- In 1811, Friedrich Koenig, a German printer, invented a steam-powered printing press.

- In 1826, Joseph Nicéphore Niépce, a French physicist, made the first permanent photograph.

- In 1840, the American painter Samuel F. B. Morse patented his electric telegraph.

- In 1868, three American inventors patented the first practical typewriter.

- In 1876, Alexander Graham Bell patented a type of telephone.

- In 1877, Thomas A. Edison developed the first practical sound-recording machine – the phonograph.

The first photograph, taken in 1826 by Joseph Nicéphore Niépce of France, shows a view from his window. He made the photograph by exposing a light-sensitive metal plate for about eight hours.

Electricity Switches On

Electric lights lit up London Bridge as early as 1881. However, the old gaslights were kept in place – in case the electricity supply for the new lights failed.

Today, we would find it hard to live, work, or play without electricity. Electricity gives us power at the flick of a switch.

Electricity in nature

People knew about electricity as early as the 500's B.C. For example, they observed that amber attracted small pieces of straw after being rubbed with cloth. We call this force of attraction static electricity. You can generate static electricity by combing your hair briskly on a dry day. The static electricity makes your hair crackle as you comb it.

Galvanized frogs' legs!

In 1786, an Italian professor called Luigi Galvani hung a dead frog by the legs to a copper hook and hung the hook over an iron railing. Galvani noticed that the frog's legs twitched when they touched the railing. He thought, wrongly, that the legs contained "animal electricity."

In the late 1790's, the Italian scientist Count Alessandro Volta discovered what made the frog's legs twitch. He learned that the chemical action of moisture and two metals, such as the iron and copper in Galvani's experiment, produced electricity. Volta then built the first battery, and produced the first source of steady electric current.

Lighting-up time

For thousands of years, people relied on oil lamps and candles to give light at night.

- **During the 1800's, gas lamps and kerosene lamps brought light to homes and streets.**

- **In the mid-1800's, inventors tried to create light from electricity, using battery-powered lamps. However, the widespread use of electric light required not only a lamp, but also a cheap method of distributing electricity to homes and workplaces.**

- **The American inventor Thomas A. Edison developed such a method. His first power plant for generating and distributing electricity began to operate in 1882 in New York City.**

The first battery was invented in the late 1790's by Volta. He stacked pairs of metal disks – one of silver and one of zinc. The disks were separated by paper or cloth moistened with salt solution.

Michael Faraday working in his laboratory. This English scientist discovered the principle of electromagnetic induction in 1831.

Generating electricity

Two scientists – Michael Faraday of England and Joseph Henry of the United States – independently made a discovery in 1831 that led to the development of electricity as an important source of energy. Faraday and Henry found that as they moved a coil of copper wire near a magnet – or moved a magnet near a coil of copper wire – they created an electric current in the wire. All electric generators work by means of this induction principle, discovered by Faraday and Henry. By the 1840's, electric motors were operating machines such as telegraphs. By 1900, electric vehicles and home appliances were powered by such motors.

Electric motors can be small enough to power such devices as hairdriers, or large enough to drive electric trains.

In a light bulb, electric current heats a wire filament inside the glass bulb, making it give off light. The bulb keeps air away from the filament to prevent the wire from burning up. Edison's first light bulb was made in 1879. This type of light bulb is called incandescent, or glowing.

The Great Inventor

What makes a great inventor? Thomas Alva Edison (1847-1931) was one of the greatest inventors in history, as well as a successful industrial leader. Edison loved making inventions – and wanted them to benefit many people.

The young inventor

Edison got most of his education from his mother, a former teacher. As a boy he read science books and made working models of a sawmill and a steam railroad locomotive. He also had an eye for business, growing vegetables on the family farm and selling them in town.

At age 12, Edison began to sell newspapers and sandwiches on passenger trains between his hometown of Port Huron, Michigan, and Detroit. He used the baggage car of the train as a laboratory to do chemical experiments. By the time he was 15, he was publishing and selling his own newspaper.

Edison listens to an early version of the phonograph. The machine recorded sound on a metal cylinder wrapped in tinfoil and then played the sound back.

Telegraph innovator

In 1863 Edison started work as a telegraph operator. Despite increasing difficulty with his hearing, he mastered the art of receiving news reports by telegraph. He made improvements to the telegraph equipment, and while working in New York City in 1869, he improved the stock tickers used to report the purchase and sale of company stocks. He set up a company to make stock tickers, and was joined by other mechanically talented associates.

Edison's own hearing difficulties made him keen to make the telephone transmit sound more clearly. He developed the carbon transmitter, still used in modern telephones.

The Wizard of Menlo Park

In 1876, Edison built himself a laboratory at Menlo Park, south of Newark, New Jersey. He tinkered with the "speaking telegraph," as the newly invented telephone was called, and invented a machine for recording and playing back sounds – the phonograph. Edison himself made the first recording – of "Mary had a little lamb" – in 1877. The phonograph made Edison world famous as the Wizard of Menlo Park.

Edison then began to work on electric lighting, and by 1879 he and his researchers had successfully tested an incandescent light bulb. Electric light was a novelty at first because few homes and businesses had electricity. Edison began experimenting to produce electricity cheaply, and by the 1890's hundreds of communities throughout the world had Edison power stations.

Motion pictures

In 1886, Edison moved to a new and much larger laboratory at Llewellyn Park, New Jersey, where there was space for chemical, mechanical, and electrical experiments. A meeting with British-born photographer Eadweard Muybridge inspired Edison to investigate moving pictures recorded on film. He and his research team invented the peephole kinetoscope, a coin-operated machine that showed a short movie through a peephole or eyepiece. They made a motion-picture camera and projector, and set up the first film studio.

Edison went on inventing all his life. He obtained 1,093 United States patents, the most ever issued to one person by the U.S. patent office. Edison believed in working long and hard. He said, "Genius is 1 percent inspiration and 99 percent perspiration."

Edison's first light bulb used burned sewing thread as a filament. This is a copy of that historic first bulb.

What will it do?

Edison's phonograph was so unusual that at first no one knew what to do with it.

- **Edison thought it would be useful as a dictating machine.**

- **He also used it in toys, such as talking dolls and children's pianos.**

- **People later had the idea of selling musical recordings for the phonograph, and Edison began to make his own recordings.**

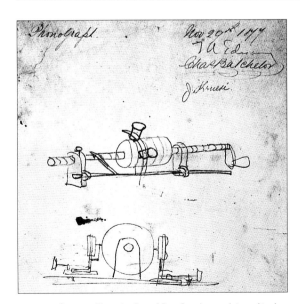

A page from Edison's sketchbooks shows his cylinder phonograph. Edison made notes on his experiments.

Waves Through Space

An early radio set of the 1920's was pedal-powered. Such radios were used to transmit messages from isolated farms in Australia.

Few inventions have changed our lives more than the telephone, radio, and television.

Calling Mr. Watson

In 1871, a Scot named Alexander Graham Bell went to the United States. He worked as a teacher of the deaf in Boston, and in his spare time he experimented with a device for sending several telegraph messages at once over one wire. On June 2, 1875, one of the metal reeds in this device stuck. Bell's assistant, Thomas A. Watson, plucked the reed to loosen it. Bell was in another room, but heard the vibration in his receiver. He realized that the vibrating reed had caused variations of electric current. In turn, the electric current had reproduced the same variations in the receiver he was using.

On March 10, 1876, Bell was testing a new transmitter while Watson waited in another room for the test message. Suddenly, Bell spilled some acid from a battery on his clothes. He cried out: "Mr. Watson, come here. I want you." Watson heard every word and rushed into the room. Bell had invented the telephone.

Radio makes waves

In 1864, James Clerk Maxwell of Britain put forward the idea that there are electromagnetic waves that travel at the speed of light. In the 1880's Heinrich Hertz of Germany proved Maxwell's theory to be correct. How could these waves be used?

Inventors worked to find a way of sending sound signals through space, carried on electromagnetic waves. In 1895, an Italian inventor named Guglielmo Marconi sent the first radio communication signals through the air. In 1901, he sent radio signals across the Atlantic Ocean from England to Newfoundland. The new invention of "wireless telegraphy" had begun the radio age.

Marconi with some of his early wireless equipment.

FIRSTS IN RADIO AND TV

- The first spoken radio broadcast was made by Reginald A. Fessenden, a Canadian-born physicist, in 1906.

- In 1925, John Logie Baird, a Scottish engineer, demonstrated a mechanical television system.

- In 1929, Vladimir Zworykin, a Russian-born American scientist, demonstrated the first completely electronic television system.

- Television broadcasting began in the late 1930's in Britain and the United States.

- In 1953, color television began.

- The first videotape recorder for recording a TV picture on magnetic tape was invented in 1956. By 1980, videotape cassette recorders, or VCR's, were priced low enough for people to use at home.

This blurred picture of Felix the Cat, a cartoon-strip character, appeared on an experimental television broadcast during the late 1920's.

Can you guess what this is? The first telephone – patented in 1876.

Electrical engineers developed various kinds of vacuum tubes that could be used to detect and amplify (strengthen) radio signals. The triode, a tube invented by Lee De Forest of the United States in 1907, became a key element in radio reception. By the 1920's, low-cost radio sets were being made, and people all over the world were listening to radio stations.

Television shrinks the world

As radio developed, many scientists experimented with sending pictures through the air. In 1884, Paul Nipkow of Germany had invented a scanning device that sent pictures short distances. His system worked mechanically, not electronically as television does. Electronic television was demonstrated before World War II (1939-1945), but television broadcasting did not take off until after the war. Early Bird, the first communications satellite, was launched in 1965. Satellites orbiting the earth made worldwide television broadcasting possible.

Alexander Graham Bell called Chicago from New York City in 1892 to demonstrate the use of the telephone to businesspeople.

Medical Progress

Louis Pasteur started the science of microbiology in the mid-1800's with his discovery that microbes cause disease.

Advances in medical science since the mid-1800's have brought new understanding about the causes of disease, as well as safer and more effective forms of treatment.

What causes disease?

Since the 1600's, some scientists guessed that tiny "seeds" caused some diseases. These seeds, which had been seen through microscopes, were actually living organisms called germs or microbes.

The microbe fighter

Louis Pasteur was a brilliant French chemist. He noted that wine turns bitter because of microbes that get into the wine while it is being made, and then showed that such microbes can be killed by heat. This method of heat treatment became known as pasteurization, and Pasteur used it to preserve milk, beer, and food. He also saved the French silk industry by proving that a microbe was attacking silkworm eggs and causing a destructive disease. Getting rid of the microbe wiped out the disease and saved the silkworms.

Making vaccines

Pasteur proved that many diseases are caused by germs multiplying in the body. He also showed that if microbes are weakened in a laboratory and then placed in an animal's body, the animal develops an immunity (resistance) to the microbe. He called this method of fighting off microbes vaccination. Pasteur proved that vaccination worked by vaccinating sheep against a disease called anthrax. In 1881 he began to study rabies, a deadly disease spread by the bite of rabies-infected animals, and worked to develop a vaccine that would prevent it. One day in 1885, a rabid dog bit a small boy and the boy's parents begged Pasteur to save their son. The scientist gave the boy his new vaccine for several weeks. It worked. The boy did not get rabies. Since then, Louis Pasteur's discoveries have saved countless lives.

An early X-ray photograph by Wilhelm Roentgen shows his wife's left hand and wedding ring. Roentgen's discovery of X rays in 1895 caused a sensation. Within a few months, doctors were using X rays to examine broken bones.

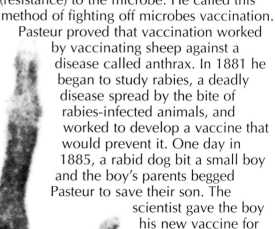
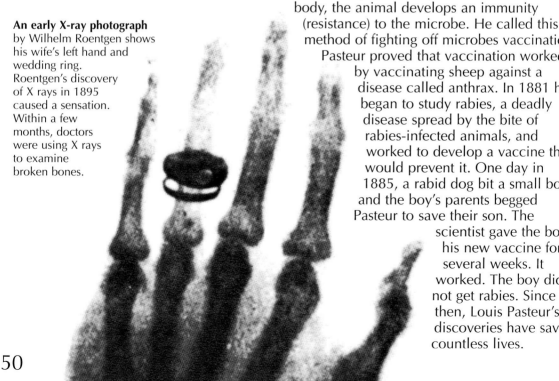

Safer surgery

Before the mid-1800's, hospitals were dirty and surgeons often operated wearing their street clothes. As a result, many patients died of infections. Pasteur's early work on bacteria convinced a British surgeon named Joseph Lister that germs caused many of these deaths. He used carbolic acid, a strong disinfectant, to sterilize surgical wounds. Later doctors used a technique that involved keeping hospitals as clean as possible, to get rid of germs. Surgeons washed thoroughly before operating with sterilized instruments, and wore surgical gowns, gloves, and masks.

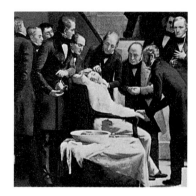

Painless surgery was made possible by the use of ether as an anesthetic. William Morton demonstrated the use of ether at Massachusetts General Hospital in 1846. Queen Victoria was one of the first women to be given the new anesthetic during childbirth.

DID YOU KNOW?

The oldest-known surgical treatment was trephining. This operation was performed in the Stone Age, when a stone instrument was used to cut a hole in a person's skull. Scientists have found fossils of such skulls that are 10,000 years old. The operation was probably performed to release evil spirits believed to be causing headaches, mental illness, or epilepsy.

LANDMARKS IN MODERN MEDICINE

1850's Rudolf Virchow (Germany) pioneered pathology, the scientific study of disease.

Mid- to late 1800's Louis Pasteur (France) and Robert Koch (Germany) proved that certain bacteria cause certain diseases.

1895 Wilhelm Roentgen (Germany) discovered X rays.

1898 Marie and Pierre Curie (Poland, France) discovered radium, used in treating cancer.

Early 1900's Christiaan Eijkman (Netherlands), Frederick G. Hopkins (Britain), and other scientists demonstrated the importance of vitamins.

About 1910 Paul Ehrlich (Germany) pioneered treatments to kill bacteria.

1928 Alexander Fleming (Britain) discovered penicillin, the first antibiotic drug. Howard Florey (Australia) and Ernst Chain (Germany/Britain) developed penicillin into an injectable form.

1950's The first successful polio vaccine was developed by Jonas Salk (United States). First kidney transplant operation (United States).

1967 First heart transplant, performed by Christiaan Barnard (South Africa).

1970's-1980's New techniques that improved the treatment of serious medical problems included computerized tomography (CT) scanning using X rays and computers; and genetic engineering, used to produce insulin (since 1982) and growth hormone (since 1985).

The Electronic Revolution

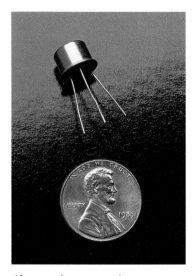

The transistor was a key invention in making the computer age possible. Transistors control current in computers and other electronic devices.

The science of electronics gives us radio, TV, and other modern wonders such as stereo systems and computers. In less than 100 years, electronics has revolutionized communications, entertainment, industry, and our homes.

Early days

Electronics developed chiefly from electrical experiments with glass tubes containing a thin mixture of gases. By passing electric current through these vacuum tubes, scientists in the 1800's found they could produce glowing colors and unfamiliar rays. These rays were shown to be made of atomic particles, called electrons. Scientists then set about inventing devices that could control an electron flow – or electric signal – and put it to work. Their experiments produced the first TV camera tube in 1923, radar in the late 1930's, and the first general-purpose electronic computer in 1946.

The first computer

The first electronic digital computer was built in 1946 by two American engineers at the University of Pennsylvania – J. Presper Eckert, Jr., and John W. Mauchly. Their computer was a huge machine with about 18,000 vacuum tubes, but it worked 21,000 times quicker than the fastest mechanical computers then in use.

Computer parts have grown smaller and smaller. Early computers filled whole rooms. Miniaturization of circuits has made computers much smaller. This multi-circuited microprocessor is small enough to fit inside the eye of a needle.

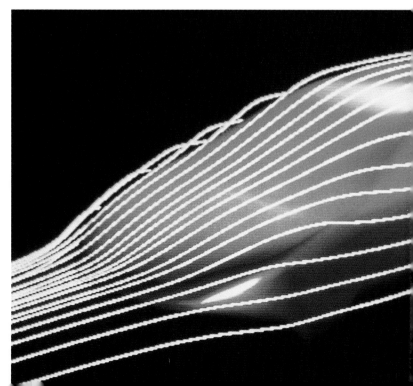

Computer games entertain children and adults.

Scientists at Bell Telephone Laboratories in the United States produced the first semiconductor diodes in the 1940's. Electronic devices made of semiconductor materials – such as silicon – could do the work of vacuum tubes using less power, and could also be made much smaller. In 1947 the Bell team invented the transistor – the semiconductor device that made pocket-sized radios possible in the 1950's. By the 1960's semiconductor diodes and transistors had replaced vacuum tubes in much electronic equipment.

Minichip marvels

The integrated circuit was one of the most important developments in computer technology. This tiny device controls electric signals. It can hold thousands of electronic parts on a paper-thin chip of semiconductor material, usually silicon. Two Americans – engineer Jack Kilby and physicist Robert Noyce – patented the first integrated circuits in 1959. By 1971 further work had produced the microprocessor, a "computer on a chip." One microprocessor may contain 100,000 transistors. Computers have become smaller and more powerful, and are now used practically everywhere.

Computers show engineers how a machine will work before it is built. This computer image is of a car being tested for wind resistance.

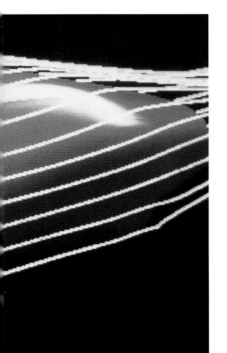

Computers can aid designers. This fashion designer can consider designs in various colors and patterns on the computer screen.

Flying High

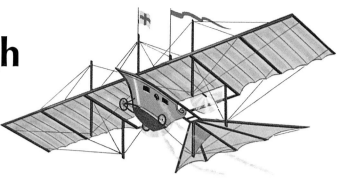

An "aerial steam carriage" patented by William Henson of Britain in 1843. It had fixed wings, and two propellers driven by a steam engine. This imaginative machine was never built.

Modern jet planes can carry passengers from Los Angeles to Sydney, Australia – almost one-third of the way around the world – in about 15 hours. Rockets have sent space probes to the planets and landed people on the moon.

From pioneers to jets

Modern aviation began on December 17, 1903, with Orville and Wilbur Wright's first successful airplane flight. By the 1930's, planes were carrying passengers across oceans.

These first planes had propellers driven by piston engines. Engineers then tried producing a new kind of engine, the turbojet, and in 1939 the first successful jet plane flew in Germany. British and American jet planes followed in the early 1940's.

By the end of World War II (1939-1945), jets could fly faster than propeller-driven planes, but not as far. Engineers worked to improve the power and speed of jet planes, mainly for military purposes. The world's first large commercial jet airliner was the British Comet, which began passenger service in 1952. The American Boeing 707, a four-engined jetliner, began passenger flights between the United States and Europe in 1958.

The Ford Tri-motor of 1926, a three-engine plane, was the first successful all-metal U.S. transport aircraft. Such planes made air travel more attractive to passengers.

Faster and higher

The fastest jets now fly faster than sound – about 660 mph (1,062 kph) at sea level. In 1947 the Bell X-1, a U.S. experimental rocket plane, made the first supersonic flight.

By 1963 the North American X-15 rocket plane was able to fly 67 miles (108 kilometers) above the earth at six times the speed of sound. Britain and France built the supersonic airliner Concorde, which began passenger service in 1976.

Concorde was one of two supersonic transports, or SSTs, that began commercial service in the 1970's. Concorde's rival, the Soviet Union's Tupolev Tu-144, was soon withdrawn. Concorde is still the world's fastest airliner.

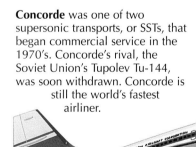

Into space

The first large rockets fired as guided missiles were launched by Germany in World War II. After the war, both the United States and the Soviet Union built rockets for use as weapons and for space research. The Soviet success in launching a satellite in 1957 set off a "space race." The Soviets also put the first person in space, when Yuri Gagarin made a single orbit of the earth on April 12, 1961. The United States built a rocket big enough to send a manned spacecraft to the moon, and on July 20, 1969, Apollo 11 astronauts Neil A. Armstrong and Edwin E. Aldrin, Jr., became the first human beings to set foot on the moon.

Many inventions and discoveries made this achievement possible. Rockets, spacecraft, computer and guidance systems, astronauts' equipment and spacesuits – all were developed by scientists and engineers working together in teams. Today, the space race is over. Scientists in the United States, Russia, Europe, Japan, and other countries are working together to build space stations and plan future explorations in space.

A picture of Mars taken in 1976 by the U.S. *Viking 1* probe. A part of the probe appears in the picture. Space probes have sent back huge amounts of new information about the planets.

ROCKET FIRSTS

- **War rockets were used during the 1800's. Some of these rockets had fins for guidance.**

- **In 1903, a Russian teacher called Konstantin Tsiolkovsky published the correct theory of rocket power.**

- **In 1926, the American scientist Robert H. Goddard launched a small liquid-propellant rocket that rose 184 feet (56 meters) into the air.**

- **During World War II (1939-1945), German scientists developed the V-2 guided missile. After the war, American and Soviet engineers used captured V-2 rockets for research.**

- **In 1957, the Soviet Union launched the first artificial satellite.**

- **In 1961, a Soviet rocket put the first cosmonaut, Major Yuri Gagarin, into orbit around the earth.**

- **In 1969, a Saturn 5 rocket sent America's Apollo 11 astronauts to the moon. Two astronauts made the first walk on the surface of the moon.**

The space shuttle *Columbia* made its first flight in 1981. The space shuttle takes off like a rocket and lands like an airplane. It will help build the planned new space station in earth orbit. In this photo, a U.S. Air Force jet flies alongside the space shuttle as it glides in to land.

The History of Inventions and Discoveries

Archimedean screw

People have made inventions and discoveries from earliest times to the present day. This list includes many of the most important. Notice how many have been made in the last 200 years.

The Ancient World

Flint tools

About 1,750,000 years ago People used flint tools.

About 1,500,000 years ago People used fire.

About 11,000 B.C. People made pottery from clay.

About 9000 B.C. People had become farmers.

Wheel

About 3500 B.C. The wheel was invented and the Sumerians developed the first known system of writing. At about this time too, people learned to make bronze by melting copper and tin together, and to fire bricks in an oven.

3000's B.C. The Egyptians developed basic geometry and surveying techniques. They discovered how to make sails, and learned how to build boats out of planks of wood. The Egyptians made irrigation devices to bring water to fields, and used a 365-day calendar.

About 2000 B.C. The sundial, the oldest known instrument for telling the time, was invented.

Egyptian geometry

About 1400 B.C. Iron began to replace bronze for tools and weapons.

About 1000 B.C. The Chinese flew the first kites.

About 400 B.C. Democritus (Greece) taught that all matter was made of tiny atoms.

400's B.C. Hippocrates (Greece) showed that diseases have only natural, not supernatural, causes.

300's B.C. Aristotle (Greece) formed theories in many areas of physics.

200's B.C. Archimedes (Greece) discovered the law of the lever and pulley, and the laws of the behavior of liquids.

Greek philosopher
Aristotle (right)

A.D. 100's Ptolemy (a Greek living in North Africa) proposed that the earth is the center of the universe. By this time, the Romans had developed cement and concrete, and made the best roads of their time. The Chinese had invented paper.

Paper

Cannon

Compound microscope

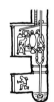

Discovery of cells

A.D. 500 to 1500

1100's Alchemy, a major source of chemical knowledge, reached western Europe from the Arab lands. The Chinese were first to use the magnetic compass, by about 1100.

About 1200 Shipbuilders in northern Europe introduced the stern rudder, another Chinese invention.

1200's Gunpowder rockets were invented in China.

About 1350 Cannon were first used in war.

About 1440 Printing with movable type was invented in Europe.

Late 1400's In Italy, Leonardo da Vinci studied anatomy, astronomy, botany, and geology.

1500 to 1700

1519-1522 The first voyage around the world was completed by sailors of Ferdinand Magellan's expedition.

1500's Ambroise Paré (France) introduced new surgical techniques.

1543 Vesalius (Flanders, now Belgium) published the first scientific study of human anatomy.

1543 Copernicus (Poland) wrote that the earth and planets revolve in circles around the sun.

Late 1500's Tycho Brahe (Denmark) observed the motions of the planets.

About 1590 The compound microscope was invented.

1608 The telescope was invented.

Early 1600's In Italy, Galileo set up experiments to find the true laws of falling bodies, and discovered many principles of mechanics. He was the first scientist to use a telescope to study the sky.

1628 William Harvey (Britain) published his book on blood circulation.

1640's Blaise Pascal (France) invented a mechanical calculator.

1660's Robert Boyle (Ireland) taught that theories must be supported by careful experiments – the basis of modern science. He also set out laws relating gas pressure to volume.

1663 The first drawings of cells appeared in a book by Robert Hooke (Britain), who pioneered the use of the microscope and discovered the new world of cells.

1670's Anton van Leeuwenhoek (Holland) discovered microscopic forms of life (bacteria).

1687 Isaac Newton (Britain) published his laws of motion.

1690 Christiaan Huygens (Holland) published a wave theory of light.

1698 Thomas Savery (Britain) built a steam engine for pumping water.

Printing press

Steam engine

Telescope

Steamboat

Montgolfier
balloon

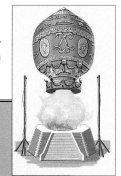

1700 to 1800

About 1700 Jethro Tull (Britain) invented the mechanical seed drill.

1712 Thomas Newcomen (Britain) built an improved steam engine.

1735 Carolus Linnaeus (Sweden) classified plants and animals according to their structural similarities, laying the foundation for modern scientific classification.

1752 Benjamin Franklin (America) proved that lightning was electricity.

1766 Henry Cavendish (Britain) identified the gas hydrogen as an element.

1769-1770 Nicholas-Joseph Cugnot (France) built two steam-powered road vehicles.

1770's Carl Scheele (Sweden) and Joseph Priestley (Britain) discovered oxygen. James Watt (Britain) developed improved steam engines. New machines for spinning and weaving textiles were invented.

1777 By this date, Antoine Lavoisier (France) had discovered the nature of combustion or burning. He also proved that water consists of hydrogen and oxygen.

1781 William Herschel (Britain) discovered the planet Uranus, the first of the three most distant planets to be identified. The other six planets had been known since ancient times.

1783 Two Frenchmen made the first flight in a balloon.

1790's Count Volta (Italy) made the first battery.

1793 Eli Whitney (United States) made his cotton gin.

1796 Edward Jenner (Britain) gave the first vaccination, against smallpox.

1800 to 1900

1801 Richard Trevithick (Britain) developed a four-wheeled steam carriage. Robert Fulton (United States) built a working submarine.

1803 John Dalton (Britain) proposed his atomic theory about the structure of matter.

1807 Robert Fulton built the first commercially successful steamboat.

1818 Britain launched the first all-iron sailing ship.

Early 1820's Charles Babbage (Britain) began to develop mechanical computers.

1825 The first public steam-hauled railroad began operating, in Britain.

1826 The first photograph was taken, in France.

1830 Charles Lyell (Britain) showed that the earth has changed slowly through the ages.

Cotton gin

Spinning
jenny

Steam
locomotiv

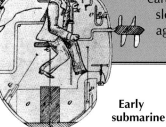
Early
submarine

Mechanical reaper

Internal-combustion engine

1831 Cyrus McCormick (United States) built the first mechanical reaper.

Early 1830's Michael Faraday (Britain) and Joseph Henry (United States) independently produced electricity with magnetism.

1836 The first screw propellers were developed to drive steamboats.

1837 Samuel Morse (United States) demonstrated his electric telegraph.

1838-1839 Matthias Schleiden and Theodor Schwann (Germany) proposed that the cell is the basic unit of life.

1840's First use of ether, the first practical anesthetic.

1845 The *Great Britain*, designed by Isambard Kingdom Brunel, became the first propeller-driven ship to travel across the Atlantic Ocean.

Mid-1800's Louis Pasteur (France) founded modern microbiology, with his studies of germs as the causes of disease. Gregor Mendel (Austria) discovered the basic laws of heredity, devising the theory of genes from studies of pea plants.

1856 Sir William Perkin (Britain) made the first synthetic (artificial) dye.

1859 Charles Darwin (Britain) set forth his theory of evolution in *The Origin of Species.*

1860 Patent for an internal-combustion engine, by Jean Joseph Étienne Lenoir (France).

1864 James Clerk Maxwell (Britain) published his elecromagnetic theory of light.

1869 Dmitri Mendeleyev (Russia) published his periodic table of the elements.

1870 Celluloid, the first synthetic plastic material to be sold widely, was invented by John W. and Isaiah Hyatt (United States).

1876 Alexander Graham Bell, a Scot living in the United States, invented the telephone.

1877 Thomas A. Edison (United States) invented the phonograph.

1879 Edison and Joseph Swan (Britain) independently invented the electric light bulb.

1885 Gottlieb Daimler and Karl Benz (Germany) built the first automobiles.

1895 Wilhelm Roentgen (Germany) discovered X rays. The first public showing of motion pictures took place in Paris, France. The first radio signals were sent by Marconi (Italy).

1896 Antoine Becquerel (France) discovered natural radioactivity.

1897 The first steam-turbine ship, the British *Turbinia*, was demonstrated.

1898 Marie and Pierre Curie (Poland/France) discovered the element radium. Marie Curie became famous for her research on radioactivity.

Telegraph

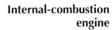

Electric light

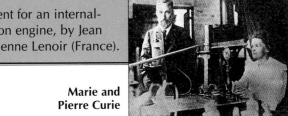

Marie and Pierre Curie

Early car

Helicopter

Jet airplane

1900 to the Present

1901 Mass production of cars began in the United States. Radio signals were sent across the Atlantic Ocean for the first time.

Wright brothers

1903 Orville and Wilbur Wright (United States) made the world's first airplane flight.

1905 Albert Einstein (Germany) published his special theory of relativity, offering new ways of thinking about space and time. In 1915, Einstein announced his general theory of relativity, about gravitation, which predicted the existence of black holes.

Frozen foods

1907 Paul Cornu (France) built a helicopter that flew but was not developed.

1909 Bakelite, an early plastic, was invented by Leo Baekeland (Belgium).

1920's Frozen foods were invented.

Late 1920's Movies with synchronized sound replaced silent movies.

1928 Alexander Fleming (Britain) discovered penicillin, the first antibiotic drug.

1929 Edwin Hubble (United States) demonstrated that the universe is expanding, as predicted by Einstein. Electronic television was demonstrated for the first time.

1930 The jet engine was invented by Frank Whittle (Britain). The first jet-engine plane flew in Germany in 1939.

1931 Karl Jansky pioneered the radio telescope.

1930's Four important plastics – acrylics, nylon, polystyrene, and polyvinyl chloride (PVC or vinyl) – came into use.

Mid-1930's Radar was developed. Much early work on radar was done by Robert Watson-Watt (Britain).

Late 1930's The ballpoint pen was invented.

1938 The photocopier was invented by Chester Carlson (United States).

1942 In the United States, Enrico Fermi and his team achieved the first controlled nuclear chain reaction.

1945. The first atomic bombs were exploded. Nuclear power plants began generating electricity in the 1950's.

1946 The world's first electronic computer began working, in the United States.

1947 The transistor was invented in the United States.

Television

Transistor

Penicillin mold

DNA structure

Satellite

1953 James Watson (United States) and Francis Crick (Britain) proposed a model of the molecular structure of deoxyribonucleic acid (DNA), the hereditary material in chromosomes.

1954 The first successful organ transplant, of a kidney, was performed in the United States.

1956 Videotape recording was invented.

1957 The Soviet Union launched the first artificial satellite.

1959 The modern form of the air cushion vehicle or hovercraft was invented.

1960 Theodore Maiman (United States) built the first laser.

1961 Soviet cosmonaut Yuri Gagarin became the first person to orbit the earth in space.

1960's Communications satellites made worldwide television broadcasts possible.

1969 The U.S. spacecraft Apollo 11 landed the first astronauts on the moon.

1971 The Soviet Salyut 1 was the first manned orbiting space station.

1976 Two U.S. Viking space probes landed on Mars.

1980's The camcorder (a video camera and recorder in one unit) became available. Small, powerful computers became popular for home and school use, as well as in business and industry.

1981 The United States launched the first space shuttle.

1986 The U.S. space probe Voyager 2 flew past the planet Uranus, and on to Neptune, which it reached in 1989.

1990 The Hubble Space Telescope began studying the universe, from its orbit around the earth.

1990's More people used mobile cellular phones, CD's and CD-ROM's, e-mail, and the computer Internet. Researchers expanded our knowledge of heredity and the use of genetic engineering.

Compact disc

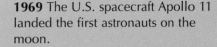

Laser

Astronaut on the moon

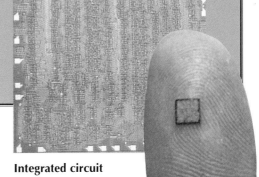

Integrated circuit

Glossary

anatomy The science that examines the structure of plants and animals.

anesthetic A drug that causes a loss of feeling in part or all of the body.

antibiotic A substance used as a medicine to kill germs or to slow their growth.

astronaut Someone who travels in outer space.

atom The smallest bit of any chemical element that has all the qualities of that element. Everything is made of atoms.

battery A device that uses chemicals to create electrical power.

B.C. Abbreviation for "before Christ." It is used for dates before the birth of Christ. **A.D.** is used for dates after the birth of Christ.

biology The science that studies living things.

chemistry The science that involves the study of simple substances or elements. It examines the way elements act, change, and combine with each other and with other things.

compressed Made smaller by squeezing together.

computer An electronic machine that can analyze, store, and give back information quickly.

cuneiform Wedge-shaped, used to describe very early forms of writing.

economic Having to do with the making and use of goods and services.

electromagnet A piece of iron enclosed in a coil of wire. When an electric current passes through the wire, the iron turns magnetic.

electronics The study of electrons in motion. An electron is a tiny particle with a negative electrical charge. Every atom has one or more electrons.

element One of more than 100 materials from which everything in the universe is made.

evolution A slow development or change; a scientific theory says that the simple living things of millions of years ago changed and developed into the more complex living things of today.

flint A very hard type of stone.

gene A tiny part of an animal or plant cell that is passed on to the animal's or plant's offspring. Genes determine the offspring's characteristics.

gravitation The natural force that draws the objects of the universe toward each other.

heredity The passing of characteristics that a person, animal, or plant has from one generation to another.

iron A chemical element in the form of a hard metal.

irrigation Supplying land with water by canals.

jet A fast stream of liquid, steam, or gas sent through a small opening by strong pressure.

lens A curved piece of glass, or glasslike material, that brings light rays closer together or farther apart.

magnet A piece of stone, iron, or steel that attracts pieces of iron and steel.

microscope A device with a lens or lenses that allow us to see things too tiny to be seen by the eye alone.

military The armed forces.

orbit The path that one planet or heavenly body follows as it moves around another; one complete trip around a heavenly body by a spacecraft or satellite.

patent A legal right given to an inventor, protecting a new invention from being copied by others.

phonograph A machine that plays records.

physics The science of how the nonliving things in nature work and move. Physics includes the study of electricity, heat, force, sound, magnets, and atoms.

pressure The force caused by pushing on or against something.

radar System that uses reflected radio waves to tell the distance, direction, and speed of distant objects.

radio The sending of sound electronically to a receiver without using connecting wires.

reaper A machine for harvesting wheat.

satellite An object that orbits a planet, such as a moon, or an artificial object launched from the earth.

sheaves Bundles of stalks of wheat.

silicon A chemical element always found with another chemical. It is found in sand, rocks, and crystals, and is used in making glass and computer parts.

social Having to do with the lives and relationships of other beings.

steam Water in the form of hot gas.

technology All the methods and machines that people have developed and used.

telegraph System or equipment for sending messages in code through electrical wires.

telephone Device or system for sending and receiving speech through electrical wires.

telescope An instrument with lenses and a tube, used to make distant objects seem closer and larger.

television Sending pictures and sounds by means of electrical signals.

vaccine A mixture containing weak or dead germs given to people or animals to protect them from the disease that those germs can cause.

vacuum An empty space that does not have anything in it, not even air.

Index

A page number in **bold** type indicates a picture.

aircraft **8**, **54**
alchemy 14, **14**
alphabet **13**
anatomy 25
antibiotics 10
Arabs 23
Archimedes 21
Aristotle 56
Arkwright, Richard 6
arrowheads **4**
assembly line **32**
astronaut **61**
astronomy 23, **23**, 26
atomic bomb 9

bacteria 10
balloon **9**, **58**
battery 44
Bell, Alexander Graham 48, **49**
Benz, Karl 41
bicycle 17, **17**
Boeing 747 airliner **9**
bomb **9**
book 24
bow and arrow 12
bronze 20

calculator 11
camera 43
car 18
Cartwright, Edmund 6, 33
CD-ROM 61
cells **57**
chemistry, origins of 14
China 22
clock **27**
communication 12
communications satellite 49
compass 22
computer **42**, 52, 53
computer-aided design 53
Copernicus, Nicolaus 26
cotton gin 7, **7**
Crompton, Samuel 6, 33
Cugnot, Nicholas-Joseph 38
Curie, Marie and Pierre **59**

Daimler, Gottlieb 41
Darwin, Charles 16, **17**
Da Vinci, Leonardo 24
disease, study of 51
disinfectant 51
DNA **61**
draisienne 17
Dunlop, John 17

Eastman, George 43, **43**
Edison, Thomas Alva 19, 44, **46**
Egypt 20, 21
electricity 44
electromagnetic induction 45
electronics 52
elevator 15
Evans, Oliver 39
evolution theory 16
explosive 8

factories 6, 32
family life 6
Faraday, Michael 45
farming **20**, 21
farm machines 34, **34**
Fitch, John 37
flying shuttle **6**
Ford, Henry 33, **40**
foundry **14**
Franklin, Benjamin 19
fuel 31
Fulton, Robert 36

Galileo Galilei 26, **27**
Galvani, Luigi 44
geometry 56
germs 10
Goddard, Robert H. **8**, 16, **16**
Goodyear, Charles 17
gravitation 28
Greek fire 8
guided missile 55
gun and gunpowder 8
Gutenberg, Johannes 24

Hargreaves, James 6, 33
harvesting 34
Harvey, William 25
helicopter **4**
Henry, Joseph 45
Hero of Alexandria 21
Hittites 31
horse 15, 22, **23**

icebox **11**
Industrial Revolution 30
integrated circuit **61**
internal-combustion engine 40
iron 14, 31
irrigation **21**

Janssen, Zacharias 10
Jenner, Edward 10, **10**
jet planes **8**, **9**, 54

Kay, John 6, **6**
Kepler, Johannes 26

laboratory 18
lenses 10
light 29
light bulb **46**
lighting 44
Lippershey, Hans 27

machine gun **9**
machine tools 32
magnetic compass 22
Marconi, Guglielmo **48**
mass production 33
McCormick, Cyrus 34
medicine 25, 50
metalworking **20**
microprocessor **52**
microscope 10
mobile telephone **42**
Morse, Samuel F. B. 42
motion pictures 47
motorcycle **41**

Newcomen, Thomas 30
Newton, Isaac 28, **28**

oil 40
Olds, Ransom E. 33

paddlewheels 36
parachute **25**
Pasteur, Louis 50, **50**
phonograph **46**
photography 43, **43**
plow 35, **35**
pottery **13**
prehistoric people **12**
printing 24, **24**, 42
Pythagoras **23**

radar 9
radio 48
railroad 15, **15**, 36
reaper 34
refrigeration **11**
Renaissance 24
research 18
robots **32**
rocket **4**, **8**, 16
rubber 17
rudder 22

Index

satellite 49, 55
satellite launcher **4**
semiconductor 53
Sikorsky, Igor 4
silk 22
smallpox 10
sound recording 47
space shuttle **55**
space travel 55
spinning jenny 32
spinning mule **33**
stagecoach **15**
steam engine 15, 30, 32
steam locomotive **37**
steam road vehicles 38, 39
steamship 36
Stephenson, George 37
Stevens, John 37
stirrup 23
Stone Age 13, 20
stone tools **13**
submarine 36, **58**
Sumerians 13
supermarket **11**
supersonic flight 54
surgery 51
Symington, William 37

tank 9
telegraph 42
telephone **42**, **46**, 49
telescope 27, **27**, **29**
television 49
textile machinery 6, 33, **33**
tractor **34**, 35
traffic jam **41**
transistor 18, **18**, **52**
Trevithick, Richard 37
truck **41**
Tsiolkovsky, Konstantin 55
turbine 21

vaccination 10
vacuum cleaner 11
Vesalius, Andreas 25
Volta, Count Alessandro 44

wagon **5**, **20**
water pump 21
Watt, James 31
wheel **4**, **20**
wheelbarrow 22, **22**
Whitney, Eli 7, **7**
World Wars I and II 9
Wright, Orville and Wilbur 16
writing **12**

X rays **50**

Picture acknowledgments

1 Model of a DNA molecule, Ryland Loos from Francis H. C. Crick, the Salk Institute. 4 Jeffrey V. Kalin; NASA; Sikorsky Aircraft; Bell Helicopter Textron Inc. 5 Detail from the Bayeux Tapestry, Bayeux Museum, France (Giraudon); Brown Brothers; 6 Science Museum, London; Blackburn Museums & Art Gallery, England; engraving (1791) by William Hincks, Granger Collection. 7 Detail of an engraving (1869) in *Harper's Weekly* based on a drawing by William L. Sheppard (Library of Congress); U.S. National Museum of History and Technology; Brown Brothers. 8 rockets from *Rocketry and Space Exploration* by Andrew G. Haley © 1958 by Litton Educational Publishing, Inc.; photo © National Geographic Society, courtesy Esther C. Goddard. 9 Heeresgeschichtliches Museum, Vienna. 10 Bettmann Archive; Merck & Co. Inc. 11 Granger Collection; WORLD BOOK photo by Dan Miller; WORLD BOOK photo; Republic Steel Corp. 12 Deutsches Museum, Munich, Germany. 14 Granger Collection; *Forging the Shaft: A Welding Heart* (1877), an oil painting on canvas by John Ferguson Weir, The Metropolitan Museum of Art, New York City, Gift of Lyman G, Bloomingdale, 1901. 15 Historical Pictures Service; Granger Collection; Mansell Collection. 16 Culver; Brown Brothers; United Press International. 17 WORLD BOOK illustrations by Patricia J. Wynne, adapted from *Darwin's Finches* by David Lack, used with permission of Cambridge University Press; SEF/Art Resource; Historical Pictures Service; Culver. 18 Arvin Calspan Corporation; David R. Frazier; Bell Laboratories. 19 ZEFA; National Park Service, Edison National Historic Site; Brent Groth. 20 SCALA/Art Resource; The Metropolitan Museum of Art, Rogers Fund, 1931. 21 Detail from a copy of a wall painting (about 1275 B.C.), Metropolitan Museum of Art, New York City, Egyptian Expedition, Rogers Fund, 1930; Granger Collection. 22 Unglazed clay jar (about 1200 B.C.), Freer Gallery of Art, Smithsonian Institution, Washington, D.C.; engraving of compass (1597) by an unknown artist, Historical Pictures Service. 23 Detail from an illuminated manuscript, *The Hours of the Virgin* (1515); Pierpoint Morgan Library, New York City; Granger Collection; Metropolitan Museum of Art, Rogers Fund, 1913. 24 Bettmann Archive; detail of an ink drawing, Ambrosian Library, Milan, Italy. 26 Culver. 27 Museo della Scienza, Florence (SCALA from Art Resource); Granger Collection. 28 Oil painting on canvas (about 1726) by an unknown artist; National Portrait Gallery, London. 30 Engraving (late 1700's) by Wilson Lowry after a painting by G. Robertson, British Museum, London (Mansell Collection); Bettmann Archive. 31 Illustration of 1788 engine, Granger Collection. 32 David Franklin, *Time* Magazine; Ford Motor Company; Bettmann Archive. 33 Culver. 34 Detail of an engraving from *Horse-Hoeing Husbandry* (1731) by Jethro Tull, Historical Pictures Service; engraving (1800's) by an unknown American artist, Culver; detail of a photograph (about 1906) taken near Beloit, Wis., State Historical Society of Wisconsin. 35 John Deere; Historical Pictures Service. 36 Granger Collection; *Clermont* courtesy of the New York Historical Society, New York; lithograph by Engelmans, *La Vie du Rail* magazine, Paris (also p. 37). 37 Drawing (about 1808) by an unknown artist, Bettmann Archive. 38 Smithsonian Institution. 39 Model in Smithsonian Institution, Washington, D.C. 40 Oil painting on canvas (early 1950's) by Norman Rockwell, Henry Ford Museum and Greenfield Village, Dearborn, Mich.; Culver, 41 Mercedes-Benz, Motor Vehicle Manufacturers Association; Culver. 42 Granger Collection, Smithsonian Institution; Paul Barton, The Stock Market; © Paul Robert Perry. 43 George Eastman House, Rochester, N.Y., The Gernsheim Collection, University of Texas at Austin. 44 Mary Evans Picture Library, Bettmann Archive.45 Royal Institution, London; WORLD BOOK photos by Ralph Brunke. 46 Bettmann Archive; telephone from the collections of the Henry Ford Museum and Greenfield Village. 47 Museum of Science and Industry, Chicago (WORLD BOOK photo by Chris Stanley); National Park Service, Edison National Historic Site. 48 National Library of Australia; Culver. 49 AT & T; RCA; American Telephone and Telegraph Company. 50 Granger Collection; Wellcome Historical Medical Museum, London. 51 Detail of a mural (1893) by Robert Hinckley, Boston Medical Library.52 WORLD BOOK photo by Steven Spicer; Science Source/SPL from Photo Researchers; © Hank Morgan, Photo Researchers. 53 © James Wilson, Woodfin Camp Inc.; 55 NASA; Uniphoto. 56 Granger Collection; fresco (1510-1511), The Vatican, Rome (SCALA/Art Resource). 58 U.S. Navy. 59 Culver; Wide World.60 Culver; Abbott Laboratories. 61 Ryland Loos from Francis H. C. Crick, the Salk Institute; RCA Pulsar (WORLD BOOK photo); NASA.

Illustrations

By WORLD BOOK artists including Robert Addison, Bill Anderson, Nathan Greene, Richard Hook, Jackson-Zender, Laura Lee Lizak, Tak Murakami, Oxford Illustrators.